Embracing Rebellion

If you can raise teenagers, you can lead anyone!

Steven L. Anderson, Ph.D., MBA

Author of *The Call to Authenticity*

Also by Steven L. Anderson:

The *Call to Authenticity*
Published by DreamStar Press
Available on Amazon.com

Published by:

DreamStar Press, Inc.
3805 N. High St., Suite 310
Columbus, Ohio 43214
614-784-8530

ISBN number 0-9755015-1-8

Author: Steven L. Anderson
Title: Embracing Rebellion

Printed by:

Perfection Press, Inc.
1200 Industrial Dr.
Logan, Iowa 51546
800-334-2920

Dedication

For Molly and Julie

Thank you for the love and insight you have given
me.
Being your father has been the most
rewarding experience in my life.

Acknowledgements

I would like to acknowledge the support I received from the following individuals in writing this book.

*My wife, Charlisa, the most amazing woman I have ever met. Thank you for your support and encouragement in this project and your help as chief editor of this book. You are the wind beneath my wings.

*My children, Molly and Julie, and my step-children, Shad, Rishanna, Tristan, and Shelley, for being an endless source of amazement and satisfaction in my life.

*My dad, for letting me tell some pretty rough stories about him in this book. I love you!

*My step-mom, for taking such good care of me.

*To Larry Anderson, Clark Powell, Jason Janoski, Terry Cracraft, Chuck Anderson, Paula Butterfield, Patrick Florence, Jim Anderson, and Molly Anderson, who all gave me invaluable help editing this book.

*My friends and colleagues, who have taught me so much about the fields of psychology and consulting, including Paul Anderson, Bob Anderson, Jonathan Hulsh, Adam Minton, Jeff McClain, Patti Hathaway, Mike McCartney, Jeff Young, Ann Fox, John Carpenter, and John Miller.

*Henry Leuchter, M.D. You are the most important mentor I have ever had.

*All the clients I have had the privilege to work with. It has been an honor to be allowed to become a part of your journey.

*The village that raised me. Thanks to all of my extended family for your love, example, and support.

Table of Contents

Introduction

Embracing Rebellion. What an unusual title. Why would anyone want to write a book about such a subject? Isn't rebellion unhealthy? Isn't rebellion something to be avoided? Not necessarily. In fact, the more work I do as a business advisor, the more I am convinced that the secret to success is in digging deep into the most painful situations, even rebellion and insubordination, and seeking the wisdom that lies there.

Allow me to share with you how I came to have this belief about rebellion. One of my first opportunities in my career in psychology was to be a drug and alcohol counselor at a nearby university. I found working with these clients to be both challenging and rewarding. I believe that I owe whatever success I enjoyed with these clients to having clear memories of what it was like to be a teenager. As a teen, I remember how afraid and confused I was, and how much energy I spent acting like I had no problems. As a therapist, equipped with that understanding, I approached these confused students with empathy and understanding. Often, even though these young men and women were forced to see me, they opened up and told me why they felt compelled to take drugs, and how frustrated they felt with their own behavior. I sensed that these clients shared their feelings with me because I embraced the pain and frustration that accompanied their drug use and did not judge them. I also noticed that once they felt understood, they began the journey back to a healthier lifestyle.

Because I enjoyed working with these students, I decided to specialize in adolescent issues, when I went into private practice. What I learned while working with teenagers and their families is the foundation of this book. Initially, our work together focused on helping these adolescents cope more effectively with their problems. This worked to some degree, but I soon realized that when my teenage clients went home their parents were often undoing much of the progress the teen had made. For example, I would encourage my clients to talk to their parents when they were frustrated with them, but their parents would often react defensively when their children would confront them, and the clients would be right back at square one.

As I thought about why this might be happening, I remembered something W. Edwards Deming, author of *Out of the Crisis*, had once said, "There are no bad people, just bad systems." With that thought in mind, I realized that the problems these teens were having might be systemic extensions of problems in their families. Because of this thinking, before I would see a new teenage client I would speak to their parents. Before long, I noticed that there were many similarities to these discussions. Often, one of the parents, usually the father, would state that their child had a bad attitude and would urge me to get tough on them. Then statements like, "Kids nowadays have no respect for their elders," would follow.

After listening to parents explain to me how dysfunctional their child was, and having them tell me how to "fix" them, I would usually ask the parent this question: "What role do you think you have in your child's behavior problems?" This query was usually met with silence. Finally, one of them would reply "None, didn't you hear what we said? We are not the problem, he is! He/she just rebels about everything we ask him/her to do!"

At this point, I would pause and ask them, "Have you ever considered that it is a teenager's job to rebel?" I must admit, this question was greeted with a lot of funny looks. But once the parents got over their shock, we would explore the idea that the only way a teenager can establish independence is to push away (i.e., rebel) from those who taught them how to get along in the world in the first place (i.e., their parents).

Perhaps teenagers can never become adults unless they are allowed to rebel. The whole process of discovering oneself is composed of pushing against the known to discover the unknown. Also, much like a ship that must push off of the dock to move into deeper water, children must challenge their parents' teachings to truly find out what matters to them, and in the process, establish their own identity.

Once the parents began considering this new view about rebellion, I would paraphrase W. Edwards Deming and say, "Please consider that the problem may not be your child, but the system he/she is in." We would then discuss the possibility that it was the parents, as much as the child, who needed to change in order to correct this problem. Much like the canary in the coal mine who warns miners of deadly gases, an adolescent's misbehavior can often be an indicator of problems in their family.

Once the parents and I could agree on this point, we would explore the psychology of adolescence. I suggested to them that their child might feel lost, and perhaps they were rebelling out of frustration. It's like the parents had created a playpen for their child that the teenager was now outgrowing. It was necessary for the adolescent's development to expand the walls of this playpen, in order to have room to discover themselves. Since teenagers are so inexperienced at processing emotions, this phase of their lives is often disruptive and painful for all involved. In fact, because teens often struggle so much with communication, I believe that effectively parenting teens is the most difficult and important leadership challenge that exists.

Then I suggested to the parents that my role as a therapist was to nonjudgmentally enter the world of their teenager and work to understand them, not try to "fix" them. Most of the time, people are willing to change only when they feel understood and cared for. In the end, it is the clients who change themselves, not the therapist. But when a therapist works very hard to make adolescents feel understood, they generally begin to open up. Once teens feel they can trust a therapist, they often admit that they feel terribly guilty about being angry with their parents. At this point, the door to healing can be opened and constructive discussions with their parents can begin.

Once my clients felt they could trust me, we would meet with their parents. I had the privilege of mediating genuine discussions between equally frustrated parents and children. Teens were urged to share their feelings of frustration with their parents. Before the teen spoke, parents were urged to listen nondefensively to their child. These discussions were usually quite tense, as parents found themselves stifling feelings of hurt and anger.

Then, almost without exception, an amazing thing would happen. Once the teenagers felt understood, they were ready to listen to their parents. There was also a tremendous sense of relief on the part of the adolescent. They and their parents often shed tears at this point. Because the adolescent felt understood, they would start to cooperate with their parents. In fact, the teens often said they agreed with their parents, but they wanted to be difficult because the parents would not listen. After this new connection the tension between parents and children began to abate and all involved began to work together and learn from each other.

Even though I enjoyed working as a therapist, I eventually left clinical psychology and decided to start a consulting company and work with organizations. As I began to work in this new field, I began to notice similarities to my work as a clinician. Employees in the businesses I work with often say things to me like "My boss doesn't really listen to me." These employees often become rebellious, just like the teenagers had; but they do so in subtle ways that will not get them fired. At the same time, their managers often say things like "These employees nowadays just aren't motivated like they ought to be. I can't believe how unappreciative they are."

Seeing the parallels between businesses and families inspired me to write this book. I sensed that the frustrations of both parents and managers could be alleviated by understanding the concept of embracing rebellion. I had a feeling that comparing the research about raising well-adjusted families and running effective companies might be beneficial to parents and managers alike. There is a great deal of research about effective parenting that I believe applies directly to the world of business. I sense that there are many leaders treating their employees like children and wondering why they are performing so poorly.

You may be wondering: Do the skills necessary for successfully raising children really translate to business? I believe that they do. In fact in the book, *If You've Raised Kids, You Can Manage Anything*, Ann Crittenden cites a significant amount of research that supports this notion. In fact, she says that two recent surveys (one by The Center for Creative Leadership and one by Wellesley College) of successful female managers have confirmed that parenting teaches skills that are transferable to management. Also, Harold Saunders, the American diplomat who negotiated the peace settlement between Egypt and Israel in 1979, said that he could have never persuaded the two sides to accept a settlement if he hadn't been widowed and left the sole parent of two children. Saunders said that the patience he developed trying to understand his children and getting them to cooperate with each other was critical in his own development as a peace negotiator. Additionally, Stephen Covey, author of *The Seven Habits of Highly Effective People* (and father of nine children), said he learned those habits mostly by raising his children. In fact, if you read through *The Seven Habits*, you will see that Dr. Covey frequently cites his experience in raising his children as examples to illustrate his point.

If you are the frustrated parent figure in this book, you may consider the benefits of listening to those who report to you, even when it is painful. If you do this, I believe you will be very pleased with how your behavior change affects those around you. I also believe you will experience a sense of achievement, fulfillment and inner peace that will make your efforts worthwhile.

If you are the rebellious teenage figure in this book, I suggest you begin to see your contribution to the problems in your organization or home. I suggest you stop being a part of the problem and start working to be a part of the solution. Even though you have a right to be frustrated, you may have more power to correct the situation than you realize.

Finally, this book is written for all the teenagers in the world who are crying out for attention, but feel that no one is listening. Please believe that there are people who care. May you one day find a way out of your present situation to a more rewarding life.

Chapter One

Seeing Rebellion as Healthy

"Young people nowadays love luxury; they have bad manners and contempt for authority. They show disrespect and love silly talk in place of exercise. They no longer stand up when older people enter the room; they contradict their parents, talk constantly in front of company, gobble their food and tyrannize their teachers."

Socrates, 400 B.C.

Scene One

"You kids nowadays don't appreciate all the hard work we adults do for you!" shouted Steve.

"Oh boy, here we go again," thought his son, Louis; "the old, 'You don't appreciate us' speech again." "To heck with you!" he yelled. "All I did was leave my shoes in the middle of the floor and you go off on me. You're such a jerk!"

"Give me a break!" yelled Steve. "It's not just your shoes. You don't finish anything. Your room looks like a pig sty. You leave your junk all over the house, and getting you to do any household chores is like pulling teeth. You're just plain lazy!"

"Well, maybe I don't want to end up a workaholic like you!" shouted Louis. "You're gone so much I hardly know who you are. When you do finally get home you are so crabby all you do is yell at us."

"Well, you try to earn enough money to support this family," yelled Steve. "You act like money grows on trees! When I was a kid, I worked my tail off and was grateful to get a dollar an hour for it. My father taught me the value of work."

"We have enough money!" shouted Louis. "I'd prefer to move into a smaller house than to have to put up with your one-track mind about accomplishments. It seems like the only thing that matters to you is what anyone produces. You don't care about me, only what I can achieve. When it comes to school, you never have time for anything except to ask me how my grades are. And all I hear about is where I am coming up short. I seem to never do anything right."

"Well, you act like you have all of the answers!" yelled Steve. "You never shut up long enough to find out what I think. You're so sure of yourself. I am three times your age with a lot more experience and you act like I am an idiot!"

"It's not that I think that you are an idiot," yelled Louis. "It's just that it's always your way or the highway. There is no flexibility. Times have changed, Dad. And I'm not you. What worked for you won't work for me. I feel like you are just trying to force feed me your philosophy. You are so out of touch with reality. I don't live in the world you live in. My friends and I care about different things than you do!"

"Yeah, like smoking pot and chasing girls! You can't even see that your friends are taking you down the road to ruin. If you'd shut up and listen to me, I could teach you some sense!" yelled Steve.

"What a load of crap! It's always a lecture. To heck with you!" Louis yelled as he stormed off to his bedroom and slammed the door. "Well, if I smoke pot, I have a good reason to," he thought. "I'm getting out of here and go hang out with my friends and see if I can have some real fun. At least they understand me."

As many of us are aware, dialogues similar to the previous one are played out many times a day in homes all across America. What is just as sad, in my opinion, is that in a more subtle way the same dialogue is going on in businesses all across the country. So why are we stuck? Why are so many families and organizations spending their time fighting each other when they ought to be supporting each other? Why do so many bosses and parents feel that their employees or children are uncooperative? And why do so many employees and children feel that no one is listening? There are many reasons, I am sure. But one that is often overlooked, I believe, is an unhealthy view of the role of rebellion. It may seem crazy to you, but I believe leaders need to embrace rebellion in order to overcome it. The only way to surmount this challenge is to see it as an opportunity, and to grow from it.

This may seem like a strange concept. Many people think that rebellion is unhealthy. The view of many parents and leaders is that their employees and children should do what they are asked with as little turmoil as possible. Well, if one looks at history, the solutions to most of our problems are in the turmoil, not in the smooth sailing.

As an example, early in the 20th century, when biology students were growing cultures of bacteria, their professors told them to make sure that no mold was allowed to grow in their dishes because it would prevent the growth of the germs. Most students worked hard to avoid this problem. But one had the courage to ask if the mold wasn't really a problem after all, but the solution to another problem. Thus, penicillin was born and millions of lives were saved by someone who had the courage to see the problem as a solution. I believe that leaders would benefit from embracing turmoil, not trying to squash it. It is often our discomfort with the messiness of these situations, that prevents us from leading effectively.

I ask you to think back for a moment to the argument between the father and son at the beginning of this chapter.

17

Why are these two fighting? Is the father right? Does the son have an attitude problem? Probably, but it's follow the leader. In the scenario I described, the adult was acting as much like a teenager as his son was. Neither one was leading. This type of fight cannot be resolved. In fact, in some families I have worked with, this situation would have ended up in a physical confrontation. In many companies, it would eventually end in a firing. In both situations, I believe, the leader missed an opportunity to resolve the situation and grow from it. Far from being a problem, I believe that there is opportunity for the leader who embraces rebellion.

For example, take the civil rights movement instituted by Martin Luther King, Jr. He spearheaded a rebellion whose time was long overdue. He had the courage to start a rebellion, that challenged the status quo. Things got quite painful for our country while Dr. King led this rebellion, but because the leaders of our country finally embraced this rebellion, our society was changed for the better.

Conversely, in the French revolution of 1789, the peasants had been complaining for years about horrific treatment, but the aristocracy would not listen. In that time, the royalty were living lives of opulence, while the peasants starved. France's leaders knew the poor were desperate, but did nothing to address this situation. In fact, anyone who even complained about the inequities of that society was thrown in jail. The leadership tried to squash the rebellion instead of listen to it. In the end, the leaders paid with their lives for their unwillingness to listen, to embrace this challenge.

If you think about it, our country was built upon rebellion. That is the power of our democracy and our nation. Allow me to quote from the Declaration of Independence. *We hold these truths to be self-evident, that all men are created equal, that they are endowed by their Creator with certain unalienable rights, that among these are life, liberty, and the pursuit of happiness. That to secure these rights,*

18

governments are instituted among men, deriving their just
powers from the consent of the governed. That whenever any
form of government becomes destructive of these ends, it is
the right of the people to alter or to abolish it, and to institute
new government, laying its foundation on such principles and
organizing its powers in such form, as to them shall seem
most likely to effect their safety and happiness.

The Declaration of Independence invites our own
people to overthrow the government if it does not work to
insure their life, liberty, and the pursuit of happiness.
Amazing! I believe that if all parents and leaders behaved
according to this same principle it would solve many of our
society's problems.

I ask you to look at rebellion from the viewpoint of
your employees or children. Not allowing rebellion is like
creating a Procrustean bed for your employees and your
children. Procrustes was a mythological figure in ancient
Greece. He was the caretaker of a cave high in the mountains
between two cities. Travelers had to stay in his cave on the
two-day journey between cities. All travelers slept in the
same-size beds. If the traveler was too short for the bed,
Procrustes stretched them out. If they were too tall, he lopped
off their feet. I feel that too many leaders have a "one size fits
all" mentality, just like Procrustes. When members of the
family or team don't fit into the mold they are not allowed to
challenge the system. They are forced into a mold, which
harms them and the organization of which they are a part.

In healthy organizations, rebellion is seen as a way to
find new and creative solutions to problems. At 3M, for
instance, employees are expected to spend fifteen percent of
their time "bootlegging," that is, doing activities not included
in their job descriptions. What at face value may seem absurd
has resulted in a very creative organizational climate. In fact,
this policy has resulted in many of 3M's inventions.

Organizations that do not allow rebellion soon become stale and flounder. An example of this is Borden. When I was getting my MBA in the early 1990s, several Borden managers were teaching where I was attending class. They told us students that they felt Borden had developed a culture where disagreement was not allowed. Apparently, Borden's top management emphasized "not failing" instead of encouraging creative thinking. As a result, Borden became stale and is now only a shadow of the great company it once was.

Research on parenting also indicates that this "one size fits all" philosophy does not work. How often do you see a family where several of the children thrive and one or two take the wrong path and get into trouble? Many people, including the parents, will often blame the child for this, which just adds a greater burden to that child. Effective parents have flexible leadership styles that allow children to rebel against the system and encourage them to design solutions that work for them; in essence, find their own identity. Let me be clear about this: if your child or employees are angry and frustrated, I believe it is your job as a leader to resolve this situation. That is where you really earn your title as leader.

One of the reasons that I feel so strongly about being flexible when parenting children is that as a child, I was not allowed to rebel. When my father was upset with me, I felt like I was in the military. In fact, he used to say to us, "Stand at attention when I talk to you, like we did in the Navy." I thought to myself, "What's good for the Navy may not be good for a ten year old," but I didn't dare say it. When I tried to give my input, he would say, "This is a dictatorship, not a democracy!" Yikes! He scared me to death.

I want to make it clear that my dad was a good father. He loved me very much. We spent long hours doing things together when I was young. He is probably the main reason I believe in myself so much today. But he definitely was not comfortable with rebellious behavior. In his defense, he was a product of his generation. He parented me the way his father parented him. In fact, he was probably much gentler than his father. I recall once hearing that my Uncle Bob, who flew a P-51 in WWII, called home after the war and informed his father that he liked flying and intended to stay in the Air Force. "Like hell!" his father boomed. "Get home, we have concrete to pour!" Wow! Interestingly, it took my uncle another twenty-five years after that to realize he did not want to work for his father's business. At age fifty he left his father's business and started his own company. Wouldn't it have been better for everyone involved if my uncle had been allowed to challenge his father and find his own path as a young man? At any rate, I grew up believing that not rocking the boat was the way to be a good team player. I learned to repress any anger I felt. This had grave results for me later on in life.

Sadly, when I was fourteen my mother passed away from cancer. As you can imagine, this caused a huge emotional upheaval in my life; but because it was inappropriate to display negative emotions in our family I did not grieve my mother's death properly. A year after my mother's death, my father remarried. In addition to having a new mother, there were four new step-children living in our home. I think we all would agree, it was utter chaos. Because we weren't allowed to rebel, many feelings that should have been processed were not.

When I went away to college things only got worse. Because I had developed the belief that rebellion was a bad thing, I did not fit in on a college campus. My peers seemed to be rebelling against everything in sight and their behavior often shocked me. For example, I can recall coming back from class one day. Several people in my dormitory were using hammers to smash the furniture in the lounge into a thousand pieces. I was shocked; clearly this was not healthy rebellion! I asked them why they were doing this. They informed me that the cleaning lady was lazy and they were going to teach her a lesson. I couldn't believe what I was seeing and hearing! Watching my peers behave like this made me feel very upset. I was convinced the human race was on the road to ruin. Because I was convinced rebellion was unhealthy and because I had no way to process my negative emotions I became very depressed in college. Over time, the situation got so bad, that I wasn't sure I wanted to be alive.

Fortunately, at the age of twenty-six, after many years of struggle, I found a very talented psychiatrist, Henry Leuchter, M.D., who helped turn my life around. As a part of my therapy, he directly confronted my beliefs about rebellion. He told me that not only is rebellion healthy, it is necessary for a person's development. I really fought him about this idea early in therapy, because it had always seemed to me that rebellion just caused anarchy. In fact, when I was growing up I used to agree with the statement, "My country right or wrong." Now I think that is as silly as the statement, "My spouse drunk or sober." In time I came to realize that there is a time to make a stand for what you believe in; to rebel against the status quo. To be effective, I believe that leaders should understand that rebellion energizes and revitalizes families, organizations, and even nations.

As I said, working with Dr. Leuchter really challenged my thinking. He once told me that leaders who don't allow rebellion in any form are usually insecure and weak. He also told me that rebellion in adolescence was critical to one's development. Unless one was able to push off from their parents, they would be unable to truly discover their own set of beliefs.

He also pointed out that there were healthy ways and unhealthy ways to rebel. So there I was, in my mid-twenties, going through the rebellion I probably should have gone through in my teens. I'm sure my parents thought I was nuts, but it had to be done. After I had completed my rebellion, I was amazed at how different my beliefs were from my parents.

22

I was also delighted to realize that I felt happy and free for the first time in my life.

So, why do so many leaders treat rebellion like it is a bad thing? In general, I think it is a combination of clinging to old-school thinking and insecurity. We need to understand that what worked in the past does not always work today. In this global economy we can compete only if members of our organizations are allowed to speak up, even rebel. If people are going to take ownership in their organizations they must have a say in how these organizations are run.

As I said, I believe insecurity is a big reason leaders avoid embracing rebellion. Some managers are too afraid of what they will hear if they listen to criticism. It takes a great amount of courage and patience to listen to someone who is unhappy with you, but courage is a critical ingredient for effective leadership. Often when I am hired as a consultant, the leader who hires me tells me that his employees are not motivated. When I ask him/her what his/her part in this problem is, I usually get a blank stare. Almost without exception, when I talk to the employees about why they do not feel motivated it is because they do not feel listened to. In my work with organizations and families I encourage authentic communication. I encourage the employees to take responsibility to speak up and tell the truth. I encourage leaders to courageously listen to their employees. I have found that when people in organizations communicate with each other in this fashion, they can tackle any of the other problems that they have.

Often the problem in leaders is not a lack of courage, but a lack of awareness. Many managers have told me that they never realized that fear and insecurity was preventing them from listening to criticism from their employees. Further, they say that they cannot believe how much they learned when they finally chose to listen. They often tell me that their newly developed awareness of their emotions combined with an increased ability to listen has transformed their home life as well. Because they have learned how to lean into painful situations, they now have the tough discussions necessary to get closer to their family and friends.

The employees in these organizations often thank me for helping change the environment they work in. "It's fun to work here, again," they often say. But the most significant change of all takes place within the leaders themselves. Summoning the courage to listen deeply to employees who are unhappy with you is difficult, but transformational. When you listen, you realize that it is not really the employees that are painful to listen to; it's the voices inside of you that are the tough ones to deal with. Once you overcome those voices, you can deal with anyone else. Leaders who confront their own insecurities tell me they no longer fear anything or anyone. They even seek out situations where they receive negative feedback so that they can grow. Once individuals do this, they experience a deep sense of inner peace and self-respect. Once this transformation is complete, life is never the same. Leaders who have experienced this transformation feel a power and freedom unlike anything they have ever felt. They feel as if they are flying. Problems now become opportunities.

You may be wondering why I use a word as strong as "rebellion" to characterize employee and adolescent behavior. Wouldn't it be better if they would just challenge their leaders respectfully? It sure would. The problem is that respectful challenging often does not happen if we do not encourage rebellion. Teenagers are often incapable of putting their feelings into constructive behaviors. They are made up of a whole bunch of hormones, insecurities, and concerns about whether they can fit into the world around them. Because of this, they often do not make a whole lot of sense.

What makes so many of these conflicts irresolvable is that many adults have not developed more sophisticated assertiveness skills than their adolescent children. Research by

Robert Kegan, Ph.D. at Harvard University indicates that up to eighty percent of adults spend most of their time in a mindset similar to adolescents, dependent upon others for their sense of self. Like teenagers they do not feel they can control their destiny. That is why so many parents argue with their teenagers. It becomes about who is right, instead of doing the right thing.

This problem of adults thinking like teenagers also explains why more problems between bosses and employees are not resolved. Many of the managers who are leading these people are stuck in the same adolescent mentality, except instead of seeking approval they want control. Neither works. So employees and managers, adolescents and parents become locked in a struggle for dominance that destroys the enthusiasm and self-esteem of everyone involved.

To get around this seeming impasse we must first understand that rebellion is not only healthy, but necessary for the development of our employees and our children. M. Scott Peck, author of *The Road Less Traveled*, says that many teams must go through four phases in order to be effective. They are **forming, storming, norming, and performing**. He says that some teams never gel because they fail to go through the storming phase of the team's development. Storming is a painful, but necessary step. It takes a good leader to take a team through this phase, which is essentially rebellion. It's the part of team formation where we tell each other what is bothering us, even at times getting angry at each other. This phase can be extremely uncomfortable, and leaders with weak stomachs cannot handle it. Too many leaders expect employees to just fall in line and perform.

Now, let's look at things from the adolescent's perspective. Research shows that without the ability to rebel, teenagers can never fully understand their own personalities. Psychologist Erik Erickson, Ph.D. said that human beings have to resolve crises as they proceed through life to enter the next stage of development. In Erickson's fifth stage, "Identity versus Identity Diffusion," teenagers are filled with doubt. To successfully complete this stage, teenagers must form a healthy self-identity. As they struggle to resolve this crisis, they can become moody, unruly, and rebellious. Erickson argues that parents must allow them to behave in this fashion so that they are able to work through these doubts and gain a more mature understanding of themselves. If they are not allowed the freedom to explore, they will remain stuck in this phase, possibly for the rest of their lives. If this phase is confusing to you as parents, try to remember how difficult your life was at this stage. Adolescence is a difficult, painful stage of life.

Taking this perspective on adolescence to the workplace, we see that we must allow employees the chance to rebel if they are to become effective and establish their identity in the organization. Hopefully, we want fully interdependent members of our teams. Interdependent employees are fully engaged with those around them. But the only way to interdependence is through the painful process of independence. Sometimes this requires rebellion. Employees must fully establish their own understanding of who they are on the team before they can fully engage in the team.

I must add a word of caution. I believe that the toughest and most important leadership job in the world is being a good parent. Your job is not as simple as just allowing your teenager to rebel. I think that the best way to think of yourself is as a shepherd. Allow teenagers to run around in the pasture and explore and decide for themselves what they believe, even if you are uncomfortable with the conclusions they are coming to. But when they engage in behavior that is hazardous to their health or that might endanger their survival, you must not be flexible at that point. That is where you must set firm boundaries.

So, how do we, as leaders, set boundaries? The first step in setting boundaries is understanding what matters to you.

Where do you make your stand? The second step is in setting the boundary in a kind, but firm manner. The third step is in establishing an appropriate consequence for breaking the boundary.

The best example I can think of regarding setting boundaries came from an interview I once saw of John Wooden, arguably the greatest basketball coach who ever lived. Now, Coach Wooden was very strict. He had very prescribed guidelines for grooming if one wanted to play on his basketball team. One of the guidelines was that no team member could have any facial hair. This was a very tough rule for players to follow, especially in the 1970s when having facial hair was the norm for college students. As the story goes, one player decided to test the coach on this, so he came to the first day of practice with a beard. At the end of practice, Coach Wooden approached him and said he would not be allowed on the team if he did not shave his beard. The player told the coach that he had thought about it a lot and really felt strongly that the beard was part of who he was and he insisted on playing with it. Coach Wooden's response to this was brilliant. He did not become angry. He did not insist that the player do what he wanted him to. He (Wooden) simply told the player, "Well, we are really going to miss you, but we will never lose our respect for you because we admire people with strong convictions." The next day the player was at practice clean-shaven. In the end, playing on the team was more important to the player than having his beard, but coach Wooden left the decision up to him. He did not yell at him or tell him he had a bad attitude. He did not get offended that the player was testing his boundary. He simply told the player there would be a consequence for breaking the dress code and let the player decide.

Another step that is necessary to overcome our discomfort with rebellion is to ask ourselves why we are so uncomfortable with rebellion in the first place. In my opinion, this is the key, as far as leaders and parents are concerned. We as leaders are expected to deal effectively with difficult personalities. Once you come to expect rebellion, you deal with it effectively, as Coach Wooden did. Unfortunately, we often fall short. We often act like teenagers ourselves. It is important to understand that it is impossible to lead with this type of adolescent mentality. You cannot empower or inspire other people if you are trying to control them or gain their approval.

Referring back to Robert Kegan's research, to empower people you have to move out of the Dependent Phase and into the Independent Phase. When we move into this stage, we truly begin to lead, to work from within. We are no longer dependent upon others for our sense of self. We understand that we are worthy simply because we are working to fulfill our inner calling, our passion. I would submit that the difference between leaders and followers is that leaders do not **react to** what is going on in their environments. They learn to discipline themselves and **act upon** their environments. In Gandhi's words, leaders understand that they "must become the change they wish to see in the world."

If you realize that you, as a leader, are stuck in the dependent phase, the good news is that you don't have to stay there. Once you realize that you are part of the problem, you can change it. When you blame the problem on others it is impossible to change.

Allow me to give an example from my own life. I used to try to control my children. When my children did not behave as I expected them to, I would become very impatient and start to yell at them. As a consequence, my oldest daughter, Molly began to withdraw from me. This hurt me deeply. When I thought about my behavior, I realized that I had a problem with insubordination. As I mentioned earlier, I was raised with the belief that rebellion was unhealthy. As a result, when I am feeling anxious or insecure, my old training sometimes takes over and I try to steamroll my children or others to behave as I think they ought to.

When I realized what I was doing to my own children I became very sad. I also decided to change. I sought advice from others. I read books about anger management. Most importantly, I talked to my children about this situation and asked for their forgiveness and help. When I did this, Molly broke down crying and hugged me. I asked my children how they could help me to stop losing my temper. They suggested I pay them five dollars every time I made them cry! I agreed. It was amazing how fast I was able to change my behavior and start to reason with my children once I gave them the power to talk back to me. In effect, I leveled the playing field. The results for all three of us have been deeply rewarding. I am now closer to both of my daughters, and they tell me they feel much more comfortable with me.

I want you to know that I still try to control my children and others at times. In fact, my understanding of embracing rebellion has been seriously tested in the past three years. In that period, I became remarried and was blessed with four great stepchildren. Three of my wife's children are grown, but the youngest, Shelley, was in eighth grade when I met her. When her mother and I were married, it was understandably quite difficult for Shelley. All at once, she lost much of the freedom she had enjoyed while living alone with her mother, and she lost much of her mother's time to me. Very often over the past few years, my ability to remain centered as Shelley works through this major change in her life has not been as good as I would like. What I have noticed about myself, however, is that as long as I remain in the mindset that Shelley's presence is a gift in my life and that her behavior is perfectly appropriate given her life stage and the pressure she is under, I respond in a constructive fashion. I will be the first to admit that I do not always do this. I continue to struggle with my own insecurities and my abilities as a parent. But I am thrilled by what I have learned as her stepfather.

In the book *On Becoming a Leader*, author Warren Bennis quotes Don Ritchey, former CEO of Lucky Stores. He said that in order to be a really effective leader, "You should preserve the right to say, 'Shove it!' and go your own way. That really frees you." I think Mr. Ritchey's comment applies to all of us. If employees/children are given the freedom to rebel and say, "Shove it!" I think they will become free to actualize their potential. This can only be a benefit to everyone involved.

Chapter Two

Healthy Rebellion

"Anyone can get angry, but to become angry with the right person, to the right degree, at the right time, and in the right way, that is not easy."

Aristotle

"Thank goodness, someone finally understands. I'm off the hook. It's the leader's responsibility to understand me." That's what the rebel may be thinking after reading chapter one. Not so fast. Yes, you probably have a right to be angry. Too many leaders and parents have dismissed your concerns and called you selfish, and told you that you have a bad attitude. But giving up any responsibility for the situation will not improve anything. You may not have the ability to think constructively about this, but if you do, it would behoove you to reconsider your position. You may think your parents or your boss have all the power, but that is not likely to be the case. You may have more say in the quality of your relationship with them than you may think. If you are really angry and you have a good reason, this chapter is written for you. It is likely there is a way out. I believe that there are options open to you of which you may be unaware.

Figure one might depict your present relationship with your boss/parent. Your parent or boss is in the control position, but you are in the dependent position angry and powerless. But perhaps you aren't as powerless as you think. The bottom line is this: controlling persons behave that way because they think they have to. They are like the cowardly lion in the Wizard of Oz. They must dominate you to feel safe, to feel good about themselves. So how do you deal with someone like that?

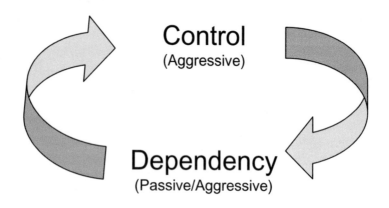

Figure 1

First of all, you might consider your role in the problem. Generally, the person in the dependent role is seeking the approval of the person in the controlling role; otherwise they would have no hold over them. It may be that you are seeking your parent's or boss's approval. It may be that you are so afraid to lose your job that you don't want to rock the boat. One way or another, if you are seeking another person's approval in a relationship, you cannot have a healthy relationship with them.

If the previous paragraph describes you, then you might consider that there is another way. To change the dynamic, you have to think of yourself as a powerful person. You have to think of yourself as a problem solver. You have to realize that no one holds the power over your destiny but you. You do not need anyone's approval but your own. In Eleanor Roosevelt's words, "No one can make you feel inadequate without your permission." In the end, it all comes down to self-respect. Once you get that right, everything else in your relationships works.

"Okay, that's fine," you might think, "but how do I get out of the dependent role? What would be a more productive way to behave in the face of my boss/parent's controlling behavior?" The answer is that you have to replace your dependent behavior with assertive behavior, and there is a critical difference between the two. Assertive behavior is different from aggressive behavior in that it seeks to heal relationships, not control others. For a more detailed description of this, please look at the chart in figure two.

Behavior

	Passive/Aggressive	**Assertive**	**Aggressive**
Confidence level	Low	High	Low
Motivation	Approval seeking	Connection with others	Control over others
Self-talk	"Am I lovable?"	"People are good, and so am I."	"The world is a dangerous place. I must protect myself."

Figure 2

Often people who feel controlled by others are moving from a position of weakness, like those in the passive/aggressive column in the chart. Unfortunately, it is often the case that they pair up with aggressive people, those in the column on the right. Those relationships are doomed to failure, as each person gets frustrated and blames the other for the problem. The only way out of the problem is for one of the people to begin to behave in an assertive fashion, to seek true partnership. This invites the other person into a constructive, adult relationship.

As I said earlier, if you really want to correct the situation, you have to see your part of the problem. As it is, you probably think of the problem as a win-lose situation. The other person is in control and you are not. They are powerful and you are powerless. You need their paycheck, their approval, whatever. In my experience, people who seek approval or control of others see the world as a place of scarcity. There is only so much to go around and you have to either control or be controlled. There are only winners or losers, nothing else. It is a model built upon insecurity.

If you feel controlled by other people, I ask you to think, as Stephen Covey suggests in *The Seven Habits of Highly Successful People*, of the world as a place of abundance. There is plenty to go around. We can all win, but we must ask, or rather insist, that we are in partnership with others. In Stephen Covey's words, we have to think "win-win or no deal." Refuse to deal with people who do not give you the respect you deserve. Stop seeing others as people whose approval you need. The only person who can give you a sense of self-worth is you.

You usually get what you want in relationships. If you have a mindset of abundance, you'll generally get what you need. If you have a scarcity mindset, you'll always feel people are out to get you. This reminds me of a story I once heard about a gas station attendant who spoke to someone who was filling up at his station. The person said that they were new in town and wondered what the people were like. The station attendant asked them what the people were like where they came from. The customer said, "The people there were incredibly kind. There was a real community spirit there." The attendant replied, "Yeah, people are pretty much like that here too." The next customer also happened to be moving in from out of town and asked the attendant the same question. The attendant replied with the same question and the customer said, "The people there were jerks. You could never trust them." The attendant then said, "Yeah, people are pretty much like that here too."

Learning to assert yourself with someone who is presently controlling you may seem ridiculous to you. If you are a teenager with a parent bent upon controlling you, you may not be in a position to demand partnership. But it may be worth your while to realize that the controlling behavior of your parents is not healthy. It comes from a place of insecurity. Someday you will not have to put up with that kind of domination. I also encourage you to try to find mentors who do not treat others that way and seek their help. There is a danger that in your rebellion against this control you may harm yourself. Guidance from wise mentors will be critical to your passage into adulthood.

For those of you who are adults, you do have a choice. If someone else is controlling you, you can get out. If you are being abused, do yourself a favor and get out, any way you can. Get a friend to help you, get some therapy if you can. Believe it or not, it's probably your belief that you do not deserve to be treated better that is keeping you in this trap.

"Okay," you may be thinking, "so I want to get out of this cycle. I want to enter a partnership. I want to get the respect and feel the power that I deserve in relationships, but what does that look like? How do I learn to set boundaries on the people who are taking advantage of me without making everyone in the world mad at me?" To be honest, it is not easy, but it can be done. You can't change years of programming overnight, but basically you have to first decide where you want to make a stand. Where do you want to set a boundary with the person who is controlling you? That is the first critical step. Only after you have made this decision can you take the first step toward achieving partnership, and more importantly, self-respect.

Allow me to share a story of my own struggle to become assertive. Twenty years ago, when I was in therapy, I was terrified to confront others, but Dr. Leuchter insisted that I start to do this if I was to continue in therapy. So, I selected my boss as the first person to stand up to. I was working as a bus boy in a restaurant, and he had been very critical of me. I felt like I couldn't do anything right. I felt angry with him, but I realized Dr. Leuchter was right, so I set aside a time at work to talk to him. I was extremely nervous and expected him to get angry with me for confronting him. I can remember standing in the hallway at work and telling him I wanted to talk to him. He then asked me what it was about. As I timidly told him how his behavior was making me uncomfortable, I could barely stand up because my knees were shaking so badly. But instead of getting angry he listened. He thought about what I had said and agreed with me. He said he would work to be more supportive of me and walked away. I was shocked.

After I confronted him I realized that the reason I was so afraid that he would get angry was because that was how my father often reacted when I confronted him. This was a significant insight to me. All at once, I realized that all those years my father had overreacted, but other people were not likely to do the same. I felt instantaneously free and extremely proud of myself. The next day when I went back and told Dr. Leuchter this story he leaned forward, raised his fists in victory, and said, "You got your foot in the door, buddy!" That was the understatement of the year. I cannot remember a more significant event in my entire life.

Once you have decided where to set your boundary, you have to confront the person who is controlling you. The only way to get their respect, or yours for that matter, is to courageously face them. This may seem foolish to you. "I'm too scared," you might think. "They won't listen," you might think. Believe me, courageous confrontation works. Gandhi once said that when you look another person in the eye and let them know that they are hurting you, and don't apologize for your feelings, it touches something inside the other person. It's how Gandhi freed a nation, and it's how you will free yourself. Ultimately, assertiveness is not an easy skill to learn, but there are many books out there you can read on this subject. There are also good therapists and coaches who can help you. I might add that it really helps if you realize that the goal of a confrontation is to get your own respect, not theirs. If you approach the situation with that attitude, you can never really lose a confrontation.

Allow me to give you some suggestions about how to assert yourself. Confronting another person is a four-step process. First, you tell the other person what they are doing that upsets you. Try to make it in behaviorally specific terms, for example, "I feel upset when you interrupt me." If you are vague and tell them they have a bad attitude, they will probably get defensive. If you do this you will just get in an argument about what constitutes a bad attitude. On the other hand, asking someone to stop interrupting you is less likely to get a defensive reaction. It's also more difficult to argue a specific point like this.

Second, tell the person how their behavior makes you feel. For instance, tell the person, "When you interrupt me it makes me feel frustrated because I feel like you are not interested in what I have to say." No one can argue with how you are feeling. Do not judge the person's behavior or call them names. If you say, "You are interrupting me because you are a domineering person," you will probably elicit defensive behavior. Don't judge them; just tell them how you feel. This makes it easier for the person to give in, because there is no right or wrong. In fact, I often will take part of the blame for feeling the way I do. For instance, I will say, "Perhaps I am being too sensitive, but I would appreciate it if you would stop interrupting me." I find that almost without exception, when I do not confront others in an aggressive tone, they do what I ask.

Third, explain to them the changes you would like them to make. Often this statement is unnecessary. When you tell someone you wish they would stop interrupting you, you do not have to repeat it. But if your boss is too critical, you may want to say something like, "I would really appreciate it if I could hear a bit more about what I am doing right."

When you confront someone it is important that you look them in the eye. They will probably take you seriously only if you show a firm resolve. Also, do not let them interrupt you or change the subject. For instance, if they say, "I know I do that, but you always...." Calmly tell them you will be glad to talk about your own shortcomings, but not until they have addressed your concerns.

Fourth, if they will not cooperate with you, do not get angry. Simply establish a consequence for their behavior. For instance, you might say, "It's your prerogative if you want to continue to interrupt me, but just realize that the next time you do it, the conversation will be over." You may be amazed how quickly you get compliance.

Remember, the toughest person in the world to confront is yourself. You have to decide that you are worth the effort to stand up to controlling, domineering people. Once you have won that fight, you have crossed a major hurdle. But, it is not an easy process. Expect to struggle. It takes a lot of practice to become proficient at it. Believe me, I have worked at it for twenty years, and I still struggle. But if you really want to learn to assert yourself, you will.

I must add that there are a few people who will not respond to assertiveness. They see the world as a dangerous place. They feel must dominate others or they do not know how to act around them. If you are working for a boss like this, I suggest that you consider getting out of the situation. Find a new job. This situation will not change. You deserve better than this abusive treatment. On the other hand, if this behavior describes your parents, find someone who can support and protect you. You need all the help you can get.

I want to end this chapter with a poem by Dale Wimbrow entitled *The Man in the Glass*. In my opinion, happiness and fulfillment all come down to self-respect. This poem has a lot to say about this subject.

When you get what you want in your struggle for self
And the world makes you king for a day,
Just go to a mirror and look at yourself,
And see what THAT man has to say.

For it isn't your wife or family or friend
Whose judgment upon you must pass;
The man whose verdict counts most in the end
Is the one staring back from the glass.

Some people may think you a straight-shootin' chum
and call you a person of place
But the man in the glass says you're only a bum
If you can't look him straight in the face.

He's the man to please, never mind all the rest
For he's with you clear up to the end,
And you've passed your most dangerous, difficult test
If the man in the glass is your friend.

You may fool the whole world down the pathway of years
And get pats on the back as you pass,
But your final reward will be heartaches and tears
If you've cheated the man in the glass.

Chapter Three

Attaining Humility

"Sit down before (attempting to change) as a little child, be prepared to give up every preconceived notion, follow humbly wherever and to whatever abyss nature leads, or you shall learn nothing at all."

T.H. Huxley

I believe that a large part of the ability to embrace rebellion is to approach the person who is upset with the appropriate sense of humility. Too often managers or parents become obsessed with success, with being right, with getting their way. Too often when our constituents rebel against us, our reaction is to get angry with them and try to bend them to our will. We quickly assume they are the problem, not us. We think they have an attitude problem. I can recall questioning my father's reasoning on some subjects as a young man and being informed that questioning him was not acceptable. This may have served to make my father's job as a parent easier, but it wasn't helpful to me. It only served to frustrate me and make me feel that my opinion had no value. As I said earlier, I do not blame my father for this, he was a product of his times.

To me, being humble means we become deeply committed to doing the right thing, not in being right. In fact I have noticed that, most of the time when I become impatient with my children; it is I who needs to change, not them. I can also tell you that I regularly struggle with humility when it comes to children. For example, I recall a few years ago becoming exasperated with my then eight-year-old daughter, Julie because she was misbehaving. I was working with my brother Paul at the time and I said, "Come on Julie you're acting like an…", "eight-year-old," my brother said. It made me stop in my tracks. Why was I expecting my daughter to act like an adult? Probably because she was preventing me from doing something that, at the time, seemed more important than being a good father. She wasn't able to act like an adult, yet I was angry with her. It was I who needed to change. I needed to change my arrogant, impatient attitude and gain some humility. If the people we are trying to lead are not following, we ought to look in the mirror first. As Stephen Covey said in *The Seven Habits of Highly Effective People*, "seek first to understand and then to be understood."

So often, our old way of thinking gets in the way of making the changes necessary to become a good leader. In my case, it was my belief that children are just "supposed to do as they are told." When I examined this belief I was able to sit down with my daughter and work toward understanding things from her perspective. It also gave me much more patience with the situation. Visually, my old view of leadership was like the diagram in figure three.

I thought my job was to direct my children, to keep them out of harm's way, to give them the wisdom of my leadership ability. What folly. This is an old school of thinking that just does not work. It is also interesting that I struggled to change this behavior for a long time, but it wasn't until I changed the way I looked at the situation that I was able to change my behavior. My new understanding is explained in Robert Fritz's wonderful book, *The Path of Least Resistance*. In it he says that if you continually find yourself repeating dysfunctional behavior it is because you haven't changed the underlying beliefs that support your desired behavior change.

Figure 3

He calls this dysfunctional pattern an oscillating system. Fritz says that if you want to create sustainable change you have to create an underlying structure that supports the behavior changes you are trying to make. At any rate, I was not able to gain patience with Julie and ultimately succeed until I changed my view of leadership from that which I have just described to the one in figure four.

The leader depicted in this diagram understands that the objective is to empower the child or employee to find solutions to their problems. These leaders help their followers take ownership of their lives. They don't feel they have to inspire this person or force them to perform.

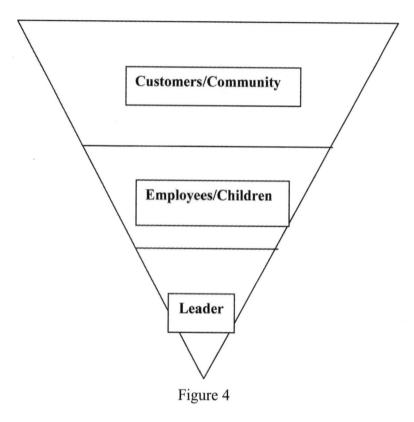

Figure 4

Since I have changed my understanding of leadership, my relationship with Julie has improved significantly, and she has gained self-confidence. For example, last fall she enrolled in a new school. Initially, she struggled to be accepted. She did not fit in and I know it was difficult for her. At one point she told me, "Dad the other kids don't really like me, but I don't really care. I know who I am and I know this will work out."

The really neat part is how wonderfully it worked out for her. Julie is a tomboy and she loves sports. Once basketball started she did really well and earned the respect of her teammates. That was just the beginning. She is a very talented runner. This spring she competed against twenty-five other schools representing over one thousand girls in the Columbus area in the city track championships. As the only fifth grader running against sixth and seventh graders, she ran a mile in six minutes and eighteen seconds and placed fourth in the city championship. Just as amazing, soon after that, we ran a five kilometer race together in twenty-three minutes and fifty-two seconds. She won the nineteen-and-under women's category in the race! This whole experience has been a tremendous bonding experience for us and a huge confidence builder for her.

I couldn't be more proud of her; not for her awards, but for her unflinching belief in herself. I am hopeful that the changes in my attitude have somehow assisted her development in this area. I believe that the key to my growth in this area has been humility.

Another way to think of humility as a parent or manager is what Buddhists call the "beginners mind." As soon as you are sure you have figured it all out, you stop leading because you stop growing. No one wants to follow someone who has all the answers. People who really know how to lead are endlessly curious. Peter Senge, in *The Fifth Discipline*, says that the most successful companies are "learning organizations." They understand that they will never fully have the answers, but they develop into their cultures a humility and endless curiosity about trying to do the best they can.

I can remember when I was a younger man; I liked to appear as if I knew everything, even though I was quite insecure. Because of this quality, I prevented myself from learning anything new and at times people avoided me because of my arrogance. Now, I am very comfortable not having all of the answers. In fact, I love the process of being wrong and having the opportunity to learn. It makes me feel alive. It keeps me humble. Fortunately, with my limited abilities, I get plenty of practice! Socrates once said, "The man who knows everything, knows nothing. The man who knows nothing, knows everything." I believe he was right.

Finally, George Leonard, in his book *Mastery* talks about humility as the ability to be a good learner. He says that in order to be a good learner you "have to be willing to make a fool of yourself." If you are really ready to be humble you have to be ready to make a fool of yourself. Then you can really learn. Then I believe people will feel comfortable telling you the truth and following you.

Chapter Four

Understanding Your Insecurities

"People motivated by fear don't build mountains. They build basements."

Mathew Miklovic

This may come as a surprise to you, but it is likely that every problem you are having with your employees or teenagers has to do with your own insecurities. Surely, your employees have done irresponsible things. Perhaps they are difficult to motivate. Perhaps there is no way to get through to them, but I doubt it. As I mentioned earlier, Gandhi once said, "We must become the change we wish to see in the world." If you are the parent/manager, and if your family/organization is not achieving the results you would like, you must be the first to change. Unless you lead, no one will follow.

So how do we overcome our insecurities? First of all, we have to accept that we have insecurities and that does not make us bad or weak. Without exception, the thing that gets in the way of our ability to lead is our insecurities. We may, at times, think that we don't have any insecurities, but we all do. It's not a problem to have them. The problem arises when we are unaware of them.

"How can I become aware of my insecurities?" you may ask. "I know what is going on inside my head." Actually, you probably are less aware of what is going on in your mind than you think. Allow me to explain why. There are about 100 million neurons in your brain with about 100 billion electrical connections between those neurons. The amount of information in our brains is almost unimaginable. Also, according to the movie *What The Bleep Do We Know?,* there are about 4 billion bits of information being transmitted in our brains at any one moment. We are aware of only 2,000 of them! As you can see, we are unaware of most of the information our brains are processing.

So, if it's that difficult to understand our insecurities how can we possibly overcome them? The answer is emotional intelligence (often called the emotional quotient, EQ), which is learning to understand and utilize one's emotions as productively as possible. To get an idea of how it works, see the diagram in figure five, which is based upon the research of Albert Ellis.

A ➡ B ➡ C ➡ D

| Activating Event | Belief System | Consequent Emotion | Dependent Behavior |

Figure 5

As you can see, everything that we encounter in our environment (A) has to pass through our beliefs (B) and then through our emotions (C) before we do anything about it (D). Allow me to illustrate; let's say we notice something in our environment (A), say a rattlesnake. We immediately access our beliefs (B) about this stimulus (A). An example of such beliefs might be, "Rattlesnakes are poisonous. I am in danger." We immediately become afraid (C), and then we run away (D).

Being a leader consists of widening the gap between A and D. Victims just react to their environment. They say things like, "I wouldn't get angry if you weren't so irritating"; or "It's not my fault I'm unhappy, I have a bad boss/husband/wife...." Leaders understand that life is challenging and they don't complain about it. When they hit difficult circumstances, they spend a lot of time analyzing B and C before they decide what to do (D). They are proactive, not reactive. While you may not be able to be aware of everything that is going on in your brain (B), you can be completely aware of how it is making you feel (C). This process of using one's emotions to gain insight into our thoughts is quite powerful. It goes beyond the scope of this book, but is covered in depth in Daniel Goleman's *Emotional Intelligence*.

If you really wish to become a powerful person who does not react to your environment, I suggest you work on becoming emotionally intelligent. If you are unaware of your insecurities, they will control your behavior, every time. So, how does one become emotionally intelligent? By far, the most important ingredient is realizing that you have been reacting to your environment and then making up your mind to change. In other words, if your actions (D) are constantly reacting to your environment (A), you are essentially a victim. If you really want to become master of your destiny, you have to always base your actions (D) on an adaptive belief system (B) that is based upon a good understanding of your emotions (C).

This may seem confusing, so allow me to give an example from my own life. I used to work with a very abrasive person, who was able to consistently embarrass me in front of my peers. This was incredibly frustrating to me. For a long time, I was at a loss to explain why he was able to make me feel so insecure. Finally, I sat down and analyzed what he was doing. Whenever I was with my peers and he entered the room

(A), I became insecure (C). I started to think about what belief systems (B) of mine were making me feel this way. I realized a few things about my beliefs. First, I realized that I was an introvert and I wished I was an extrovert. Second, this person was very comfortable socially and I was not. I realized that this person had power over me because I allowed him to make me feel inadequate because I was not as skilled socially as he was. At this point, I confronted my dysfunctional belief system (B). I decided that I could not control the fact that I was an introvert and I had nothing to be ashamed of. Having this new level of self-acceptance completely put me at ease. The next time I was with this person he tried to embarrass me, once again. I simply looked at him and asked him why he was acting so rude. I'll never forget his reaction. His eyes widened as he realized that his game was over. From that day on he never bothered me again. I was no longer his victim.

Unfortunately, becoming emotionally intelligent is a slow process that requires a good deal of work. But don't become discouraged. Once you make up your mind to change, you will follow through a natural progression toward your goal of becoming a more effective leader/parent. This natural progression has been thoroughly researched by James Prochaska and proceeds through the following steps:

1) **Precontemplation** – "It's not my fault. It's their fault."

2) **Contemplation** – "Maybe it's my fault." This step requires humility.

3) **Preparation** – "It is my fault and I am getting ready to change." This step takes a lot of courage.

4) **Action** – Doing whatever is necessary to change. This step requires a great deal of work.

5) **Maintenance** – Insuring that you do not backslide.

6)   **Termination** – Ending the process of change.

Allow me to give an example of this six-step process from my life. As I mentioned earlier, when I was a young man, my mother died of cancer. Obviously, this was a very traumatic event for me. It created tremendous problems in my development, which I was unable to resolve for many years. I thought it wasn't fair that this had happened to me. I was very angry because of all of the problems that came into my life as a result of this tragedy. I also spent many years searching for other people to provide for me the care that I had lost when my mother had died. This was, of course, a futile search that got me in a lot of trouble. During this period I spent long hours feeling sorry for myself. I became despondent and depressed. In fact, I wasn't sure I would ever be happy again. It wasn't until I found a great therapist, Henry Leuchter, M.D., that I began to overcome my tremendous inner turmoil over my mother's death. This man's courage, insight, and steadfast commitment, saw me through my darkest hours. I will be forever indebted to him.

Dr. Leuchter helped me come to grips that by not accepting my mother's death, I was preventing my own development. I was dependent upon others for my happiness. Initially, this made me very angry with him. "I have a right to my anger," I thought. He agreed with me. It was a terrible thing that my mother had died, but, nonetheless, I would have to come to grips with this reality if I were to begin to grow again. Thus, with Leuchter's help, I was able to move beyond the precontemplation stage and into contemplation. I began to realize that many children lost parents during their childhoods. In fact, I did a research paper on the subject and found out that five percent of all children lose at least one parent before they are eighteen years of age. Suddenly, I realized I wasn't so alone. I also realized that there were some people with far worse problems than me. Yes, losing my mother was an awful blow. I will always miss her, but I began to realize that the sense of dependence I had created upon others was my own doing. In a sense, Dr. Leuchter told me, I must become the mother that I had lost and give myself the love that I had been denied when she left this world.

With Dr. Leuchter's help I was finally able to enter the preparation stage, and begin to plan my way out of the mess that I had created. Once I started to listen, he helped me realize how I had made myself powerless by creating dependence upon many of those who surrounded me. He also helped me realize that the only way out of this mess was to start setting boundaries upon those who had sought to control me because of my state of emotional dependence. Thus, with his help, I began to become assertive, and I entered the "action stage." I also began to take better care of myself. I got in good physical condition and I did something I had always dreamt of, I got my pilots license. My life began to turn around because I became dependent upon myself, not upon others for my happiness. Abraham Lincoln once said, "I believe most people are about as happy as they make up their minds to be." Dr. Leuchter showed me the truth of this statement. I must tell you that I have greatly simplified this process. It was incredibly difficult and confusing. It took me three years of therapy to complete. The "action stage" probably lasted eighteen months. It finally ended when I realized there was no longer anyone of whom I was afraid. From that point on, I entered the maintenance phase of this change process. Once I felt empowered, completing this change was a simple process of increasing my ability to confront my problems and to understand and pursue my dreams.

Believe it or not, the hardest part about therapy was ending it. I can still remember the day I realized that my therapy was almost over. I was sitting in the "therapy chair" I had sat in so many times before. Dr. Leuchter was in the other room talking to his office assistant. The sun was shining in through the window beside me and I could see small particles of dust floating in the air. I felt an incredible sense of peace and warmth inside as I realized that my journey to mental health was almost complete. I was very proud of myself at this moment, but also a bit sad. I had come to treasure my talks with Dr. Leuchter and I knew I would forever miss him when therapy was over. In short, I had come to love Dr. Leuchter and I was sad that our relationship would soon end.

It may seem very strange to you, but being mentally ill was the best thing that ever happened to me. Working with Dr. Leuchter was the most rewarding, transformational process I have ever undergone. His commitment to me was total. I changed because he believed that I could and he had the skill to assist that process. I would not be a psychologist, nor would I be writing this book, had I not become sick and had the good fortune to meet Dr. Leuchter. I am now incredibly happy because of the work that I did with him. I can honestly say that terminating therapy was one of the saddest things I have ever done. I can only hope that the work I do now, in some small way helps others the way he helped me.

I hope the former example has helped you understand the change process. It can be very difficult, but once you make up your mind to overcome your problems and become emotionally intelligent, it's only a matter of time before you will succeed. In order to increase your chances of success, you may want to gain a better understanding of emotional intelligence. Daniel Goleman has written several good books about this subject. My previous book, *The Call to Authenticity* also provides some good instruction in emotional intelligence. I also recommend that you keep a journal of your emotions and the beliefs that drive them. I generally recommend that clients write about their emotions in the following manner. Once you know you feel insecure you:

1) **Acknowledge what you are feeling**
2) **Accept your feeling**
3) **Assess your feeling and make a plan of action**
4) **Act upon that assessment**

Allow me to give an example of this process from my own life. A year ago, my wife Charlisa, started taking acting classes. She really enjoyed them and has since begun pursuing an acting career. This is a wonderful development in our lives, but it has also added stress because she was already working a full-time job. By August we were both beginning to get a bit frazzled by the whole process.

One night in particular she came home totally exhausted and just went to bed. I was quite frustrated because I love to spend time with her and I felt that acting was starting to take my wife away from me. As I acknowledged my frustration with this whole process, I felt a bit selfish, but I accepted my feelings as being valid. Then I began to assess my feelings. "There is not enough time in Charlisa's life for her job, her acting, and me," I thought. My initial reaction was to tell her to cut back on acting, but I knew how much she loved what she was doing.

Then I realized that there was one more thing we could cut out of her life, her job. This initially scared me because we really needed her salary to pay our bills. But I am a firm believer in moving with courage toward what one is passionate about so I decided it was time to end the assessment phase of this process and move to action. I suggested to Charlisa that she quit her job. Initially she was also quite afraid to do this, but the more she thought about it the more excited she became. To make a long story short, she now works part-time at my consulting firm and puts the rest of her energy into acting. Her acting career is blossoming and so is our marriage. We have never been happier. I believe that all of this happened because we did not react to our emotions, but acted upon them. Instead of just getting frustrated with the situation last August and yelling at each other, we sat down and talked about it and implemented a plan that has drawn us closer together.

Another way to improve your emotional intelligence (EQ) might be to hire a therapist or coach who is skilled in this area. Also, enlist the help of others who care about you and can give you feedback on your behavior and your progress. It is also important to make time in your day to be quiet. Insecurities are like rocks on the bottom of a lake. You can only see them when the surface of that lake is calm.

I would also like to suggest that the process of developing EQ takes time. George Leonard, in his book *Mastery*, says it takes eighteen months to gain a new complex skill and about five years to master EQ. That is probably about how long it will take you to master this new skill. On the other hand, don't get discouraged. As soon as you begin to apply this process, usually within thirty days, you will begin to notice that your life is improving in significant ways. It's like weight loss. In a month you can feel that your pants fit more loosely, but it may take a good bit longer to realize your ideal weight. Regardless, any progress is invigorating and fuels the rest of the process of change.

In summary, if we wish to lead effectively, it is helpful to be familiar with our emotional landscape. If insecurity drives our behavior, it is difficult to lead effectively. On the other hand, if vision and passion drive our behavior, we have a good chance of becoming a leader who feels comfortable with any discomfort we may have to face, even rebellion.

Chapter Five

Encouraging Rebellion

"Thrust into pain. It is the great purifier."

Percy Cerutty

I love to be confronted. A lot of people think I am strange because of this, but many of the things I have learned in my life have resulted from this quality. In fact, on my second date with my wife I upset her and she confronted me about it. I listened intently as she told me why I had offended her. This discussion had a lot to do with our falling in love. I was thrilled to have a partner who had enough self-respect to stand up for herself. She was thrilled that I was so non-defensive when she confronted me. This confrontation set the stage for a wonderful relationship of honesty and trust. We have no secrets, no grudges. It may seem odd, but encouraging confrontation develops relationships devoid of tension and full of trust. I believe that when you deeply understand the value of rebellion, you will not only tolerate it, you will learn to encourage it.

The written values of our company, Integrated Leadership Systems, state that authentic communication is a hallmark of our organization. Because of this, I insist that my employees challenge me when they think I am wrong. I do not see my job as being the infallible leader who always knows what to tell my employees. I see my job as the person who enables them to provide great service to customers in the best way they know how. This means that sometimes I am going to be wrong. As I mentioned earlier, I actually enjoy being wrong, because it gives me an opportunity to learn. Also, because I do not mind making mistakes, I quickly learn from them and improve my effectiveness. I refuse to spend any time "beating myself up" for making a mistake. Everyone makes mistakes, but leaders quickly learn from them and move on. I have also noticed that when I admit I made a mistake it empowers the person who challenged me and energizes other members of the team. I also believe that making mistakes is a necessary part of leading. I agree with a statement I once heard from hockey great Wayne Gretsky, "You miss one hundred percent of the shots you do not take." If we are going to score, we have to risk missing the net.

Some managers and parents may think they have to be right all of the time. They feel they will be seen as weak if they make a mistake. They try to dominate others. They may be insecure people who think their role is to control other people and keep them in line. That behavior will only cause resentment. When I think what makes a leader effective, I believe it has a great deal to do with supporting the people around them so that they can do their best. This skill is often called empowerment. Feeling the need to be right works counter to this skill of empowerment. I suggest that managers and parents work to do the right thing, not to be right. If we are to do the right thing, we must be willing to admit we are wrong.

Allow me to return to the Declaration of Independence to illustrate this point. Before the United States was formed, no country had ever given the people as much power as the leaders of our nation did in 1776. But those leaders believed in the wisdom of the common man so much that every man received a vote. Not only did leaders do this, but they gave all citizens of our country freedom of speech and press unlike any other society ever created. It was a huge risk to take, and it paid off handsomely. This faith in the wisdom of the common man has made America one of the greatest nations on earth. I believe that model is a great way to view your family or organization. Have a vision. Give the people a say in the vision. Let them criticize your behavior. The history of our nation indicates that this style of leadership breeds greatness.

Another way to encourage rebellion is to allow others to become angry with you. Ron Wolf, who managed the Green Bay Packers when they won their last Super Bowl, said he would never hire someone unless they knew how to "pound the table." That is, get in his face and argue their position strongly enough to make him uncomfortable. Give your employees and children enough leeway to develop their own vision and "pound the table" over it.

In my opinion, the only people in any organization who make a real difference are the ones with a strong vision and the will to fight for it. Having a strong vision is an incredibly compelling and powerful force to be around. It changes lives and attitudes. I also believe it empowers people to speak their minds. The best example I can think of was in a recent biography I read about Mother Teresa. She was a woman with a vision so compelling she was ready to die for it. Because of her passion for this vision, she changed the world.

Allow me to tell a story about Mother Teresa from that book. Many years ago, she was working in the poor neighborhoods of Calcutta, but not in the poorest areas. Every day on the train to work she would see people dying in the streets. The poverty in these areas was horrible to behold. People were starving or dying of disease right on the street, covered in filth, with no one to care for them.

I believe that most of us, when seeing this, would feel overwhelmed by this misery and just turn away, but not Mother Teresa. It moved her so deeply that she decided to do something about it. She went all the way to the Pope to get permission to set up a building in the poorest area of Calcutta, with the sole purpose of giving the dying a decent place to "go home to meet God." After receiving approval, she rented an old abandoned building and set up shop with a few other nuns who were willing to help her. However, the people in the neighborhood were not happy that she had occupied a building in their area. They were concerned that she was there to win converts to Catholicism, and not to help the dying.

One day, an angry mob of neighbors gathered outside and began hurling stones at her building and yelling for her to close up shop and leave the area. Pretty frightening, especially for a five foot tall, one hundred pound woman, right? Wrong. Mother Teresa went outside and confronted the group asking what the problem was. When they told her they wanted her to leave, she told them she just wanted to give the dying a decent burial. Then she said, "If you want to kill me go ahead. If not, get out of my way so I can do my job!" Wow, what courage! With that, they could see her sincerity and they put down their rocks and offered to help her. Today there are over four thousand nuns working worldwide to help the poorest of the poor, thanks to her vision. I hope this story inspires you as much as it inspired me. I also hope it helps convince you that part of a leader's job is to help the people within our organizations develop a vision that they can become deeply passionate about. Employees with this level of passion can help our organizations become truly great.

Another way to encourage rebellion is to become a courageous listener. Courageous listening means you continue to listen and not interrupt no matter how bad it hurts. When we listen courageously, we become deeply committed to understanding what the other person is saying. Often, the things our employees and teenagers have to say to us can be painful to listen to, but if we listen nondefensively we can usually resolve whatever tension is between us.

When I was a retail manager, I occasionally had to handle customers who had become very angry with me or one of my employees. I found that if I did not get defensive and just continued to listen, the customer usually "lost all of their steam." In fact, eventually they started to apologize for their outburst if I just listened long enough. When they were through talking I summarized what they had said and asked them if I had heard them correctly. Once we agreed on what the problem was I asked them how I could make them happy. By this time, the customer was usually on my side. In fact, in many cases these customers became dedicated to shopping at our store just because I had listened.

I do not believe there is any one single thing we can do that shows more respect for someone else than simply listening to them. I have coached many parents and leaders who are frustrated with their employees or children. In most cases, the single most important challenge these individuals have had is their difficulty in listening.

If you would like to become a more effective leader, developing more effective listening skills is a good place to start. However, listening is a lot harder than it looks. In my experience, most poor listeners are unaware that they have this problem. Why is this? Usually, poor listeners struggle with insecurity. For them, talking is a form of anxiety management. It just feels good to some people to talk when they are feeling tense. Unfortunately, at the time it is most important for them to listen; they are unable to do so.

Talking can also be a form of controlling others. People who continually interrupt and repeat themselves are really saying that they do not want to listen to input from others. Verbosity can come from a view of life that every relationship is a win-lose situation. With this philosophy, there is no point in listening to someone you need to control. If you really want to become a really effective leader I ask you to look at every relationship you have as win-win. With this philosophy you realize that the only way for both of you to win is to deeply understand each other. The best way to deeply understand another persons' needs is to really listen to what they are saying.

A wonderful book about how to communicate with teenagers is *How to Talk so your Kids will Listen and Listen so your Kids will Talk* by Adele Faber and Elaine Mazlish. According to the authors, the way to convince your children, or your employees for that matter, that you care about them is to suffer on their behalf. What does this mean and what does it have to do with encouraging rebellion? It means that we are willing to get heartburn for the things that concern them. It encourages rebellion because when they know you are willing to suffer for them, they'll speak up.

The authors give a great example of what this looks like. If your teenagers come to you and ask if they can go to a party, there are two wrong answers, "yes" and "no." If you just say "yes" without thinking, they will wonder if you care about their safety. If you just say "no" without thinking they will rightfully believe that you don't care about their interests. The proper thing to do is to sit down and discuss the situation with them. Ask them who is hosting the party. Ask them how many kids will be there. Ask them if there will be any alcohol. Ask them what time they will be home. Wrestle with the situation. The research presented by the authors suggests that at this point it does not matter what decision you make; the child, or employee, feels valued.

So what does deep listening look like? Here are some suggestions. First, give the person you are listening to good eye contact. Second, lean toward the other person. Show them that you are engaged in what they are saying. Third, it helps to nod while you listen to let them know you understand what they are saying. Fourth, when they are done talking, pause for a second to be sure they are finished. Fifth, occasionally restate what the other person has said to see if you understand them. Sixth, it may help to reflect the person's feelings back to them. For instance, when an employee describes a difficult situation with a coworker, you might say, "That sounds frustrating." Bottom line, you have to work to make the other person feel heard. In the end, if people feel that you are putting effort into understanding them, they will feel valued. That is what really matters.

The idea of encouraging rebellion may scare a lot of people. To be honest, sometimes it scares me. But I believe great organizations are characterized by authentic communication that comes directly from leaders who value feedback of all forms, even rebellion.

Chapter Six

Nourishing Their Actualization

*"Two roads diverged in a wood
And I took the one less traveled by
And that has made all the difference."*

Robert Frost

Each winter I ask my children where they would like to go on vacation the following summer. When I asked my oldest daughter, Molly, that question two years ago she said, "China." Well, we did not have the finances to take the family to China, but that's not what I told her. I asked her why she wanted to go there. She told me that she loved Chinese culture, language, and arts. She also told me that she has a longing to travel internationally. After listening to this, I told her that I did not have enough money to take her to China, but I wanted to support her interest. I asked her if she had ever heard of Chinatown in New York City. She said that she had not. I told her about it and asked her if she wanted to go there instead. She enthusiastically said, "Yes!" So, that summer we spent five days in Manhattan touring the city. Molly did all of the research for the trip and we had a marvelous time. We spent an entire day in Chinatown. We both loved it. Most of all, she told me that it was very important to her that I got so excited about something that mattered to her.

Upon hearing this I asked her what else I could do to support her interest in learning about other cultures. As a result of that discussion, she spent a month in Quebec City this summer with her uncle. She had a wonderful time exploring the culture and brushing up on her French. To make this story even more fulfilling, my wife's brother moved to Beijing this year and it now appears that next summer our whole family will be going to China. I feel I can directly attribute this enriching development in our family to encouraging Molly's dreams. I also sense that the realization that she can make her dreams come true, no matter how large, is having a significant impact upon her growth as a woman and her confidence in the dreams she has for the rest of her life.

Tony Robbins, author of *Unleash the Giant Within*, says that when you dream you should to do so like a small child. If you ask a child what they want, they might say something like, "I want a swimming pool. No, I want two of them; one for you and one for me!" He said their parents would probably respond with, "You'll be lucky to get a bathtub!"

I urge you to encourage your employees and teens to dream like small children and then find a way to help them make those dreams come true. Every year, my wife and I go on a retreat to talk about what we want to accomplish for the upcoming year. We dream like little kids, and we have a great deal of fun! When we are done, we write down everything we have decided upon and hang it up in our bedroom as a roadmap for our activities for the coming year. It is amazing how many of those dreams come true just because we had the courage to dream them and write them down. It is also wonderful what dreaming together does to our relationship. This dreaming process has made us remarkably close to one another. It may seem silly to you, but I often feel like I am flying with her, soaring over new territories and marveling as our life unfolds.

More than any other thing, dreaming together with my wife has made my life a wonderful journey.

My wife, Charlisa, has also added an element of dreaming to our daily lives at the office. We both recently read a wonderful book by Norman Vincent Peale entitled *Making Positive Imaging Work for You.* In this book, Dr. Peale gives many examples of how people achieve incredible dreams simply by visualizing them and then deeply believing they can achieve them. For instance, several decades ago Dr. Peale was editor of the magazine *Guideposts.* In spite of his best efforts, the magazine was losing money, so he went to his board of directors and suggested the magazine cease publication. Everyone on the board agreed with him except for one woman. This woman asked Dr. Peale how many subscriptions their magazine had presently. Dr. Peale replied, "Forty thousand." This board member then asked how many subscriptions were needed for the magazine to break even. Dr. Peale replied, "One hundred thousand."

The woman then asked everyone in the room to close their eyes and hold hands. When everyone had complied, she said a prayer of thanksgiving that the magazine had already achieved a subscription rate of one hundred thousand. Dr. Peale said the effect of this prayer on the room was unbelievable. As soon as everyone opened their eyes, they began making suggestions as to how to increase the subscription rate. The mood went from depressing to hopeful. Also, they all suddenly believed they could achieve this goal. What is even more amazing is what this prayer did to the subscription rates of the magazine. Not only did they reach their goal, but the magazine now has over four million subscribers!

With this story in mind, Charlisa wrote a prayer that we now recite every morning before we begin our work together. It is as follows, "We would like to take this opportunity to give thanks for allowing Integrated Leadership Systems to become the most sought-after leadership development organization in the world." I have no idea how this will affect our company in the future, but I can tell you that it makes me feel totally connected to my wife and gives me confidence that we can do whatever is necessary that day to provide tremendous service to our clients.

In the book *Think and Grow Rich*, Napoleon Hill describes how he helped two thousand people become millionaires in the 1920s. He said that as he worked with people, he saw that those who succeeded did three things in common. First, they said they were going to achieve their goal. Second, they wrote it down. Third, they set a date for its completion. In my work as a clinical psychologist, I have become convinced that Napoleon Hill is quite accurate. People seem to get exactly what they expect out of life. So often, people would come into therapy quite depressed. Most of the time, just when they were in a position to really make their lives great, they quit therapy. What a shame! They got exactly what they wanted from therapy, less misery. Those who really turned their lives around had a deep underlying belief that they had something special to contribute to the world. They set their sights high, and I helped them achieve their dreams.

Therein lies a great opportunity to embrace rebellion as a leader. If one of your employees is angry with you or frustrated with you, it might be because you are doing nothing to nourish their dreams. Ultimately, people seem to get the most excited about the contributions they are making and the recognition they are receiving for it. In fact, research by Gallup in Marcus Buckingham's *First Break all the Rules* indicates that employees who are engaged at work are safer, more profitable, and more customer-focused. A big factor in an employee's level of engagement is how much appreciation they feel from their supervisor.

But just recognizing your employees or children is not enough. According to Abraham Maslow, the deepest drive in each human being is to self-actualize. When we know that we are using our God-given talents to their utmost in service of our fellow-man, we feel a deep sense of satisfaction and fulfillment. How do you provide support for the actualization of your children or employees? Well, old-school management/parenting said that children and employees really don't know what they want, so you have to tell them. In my experience, that style of leadership breeds resentment and poor performance. On the other hand, teaching children or employees to understand and harness their dreams is a difficult process. In my first book, *The Call to Authenticity*, I detailed how to do this. I will summarize that process here for the benefit of those who have not read that book.

The first stage in that process is to help them understand that their feelings are valuable. Once again, what I am talking about is called emotional intelligence. Before you dismiss the power of emotions, consider that the link between intelligence and success in life is weak at best. Conversely, the link between emotional intelligence and success in life is quite robust.

How does one show his employees or children that their feelings matter? First of all, by valuing and understanding your own feelings. Research by Antonio Damasio indicates that those who have a poor understanding of their emotions make poor decisions and have an inability to form healthy relationships with other people. Once you start to value your own feelings, you can start to appreciate those of your children or employees. To do this, you listen whenever they tell you how they feel. Make them feel entitled to their feelings.

To give an example of a leader who values emotions, I turn to Daniel Goleman's *Primal Leadership*. In his book, Goleman describes how an emotionally intelligent leader walked into his staff meeting and sensed tension in the room. He put aside his agenda and asked the group if there was something wrong. They told him about a problem that had arisen that had them greatly concerned. The leader then spent a good portion of the meeting dealing with the employees' concerns and in doing so showed that he valued their feelings. Because of their manager's behavior, the employees left the meeting feeling important and excited about how they could support their leader.

Once your employee or child understands that you value their feelings, encourage them to dream. Interestingly, many people have no idea what they really want in life, perhaps because they have never been asked. In *What Color is Your Parachute?* Richard Bolles says that most people spend more time planning their dinner than their careers. If that is true it is very sad. It makes sense to me that really leading means making the time to listen to our children's/employees' dreams and helping them come true. It also seems that employees who are striving to make their dreams come true will stop at nothing to help their organizations succeed. Really caring about others and helping them to succeed is good for all involved.

So, how do we learn what our dreams are? There are many components, but a critical piece is taking time to listen to our emotions, especially what excites us. Dr. Leuchter taught me this many years ago. Because of his assistance, I dedicate ninety minutes every Friday to meditate and listen to my dreams. In those sessions I try to get into the mindset of a child. Can you remember the way you felt as a child when you were so immersed in an activity that you could hardly sleep at night? Maybe you were building a snowman or starting a new club with your friends. That is the mindset that produces passion and dreams. Everything of significance I have accomplished has become apparent to me in those Friday sessions.

It may also be helpful to keep a pad of paper with you when you are sitting quietly. The ideas will come and you have to capture them when they do. Make a commitment to

70

yourself to find a quiet place in your life just to be still and listen. Author John Maxwell calls his place his "thinking chair," and he says it calls to him when he spends too much time away from it. Marketing guru Jay Abraham calls his time "cooking without gas." Also, I recently heard Stephen Covey say that the CEO of Chick-fil-A, S. Truett Cathy, goes on a one-day retreat every three months in a cabin in the mountains armed only with a blank pad of paper and a pen. All three men state that this quiet time is critical to their success.

I believe that our next job as leaders is to nourish these dreams when the employee or adolescent brings them to us. For instance, I can remember once hearing that the secretary to the chief executive officer at Johnsonville Brats asked him why they didn't have a mail order business. Instead of dismissing this idea he asked her to go research it and report back to him. According to Tom Peters, author of *In Search of Excellence*, not only did that company start a mail order division, but the woman who came up with the idea now leads the division. Now that's encouraging a dream!

Another way to help nourish your employees' or children's actualization is to challenge them. Don't tolerate mediocrity. Ask them to be the best they can be. The best way I can describe the idea of challenging your employees or children is captured in the following beautiful poem written by Denis Waitley. It is written from the perspective of a child.

Roots and Wings

If I had two wishes, I know what they would be,
I'd wish for Roots to cling to, and Wings to set me free;

Roots of inner values, like rings within a tree,

and Wings of independence to seek my destiny.

Roots to hold forever to keep me safe and strong,
To let me know you love me, when I've done something
wrong;

To show me by example, and help me learn to choose,
To take those actions every day to win instead of lose.

Just be there when I need you, to tell me it's all right,
To face my fear of falling when I test my wings in flight;

Don't make my life too easy, it's better if I try,
And fail and get back up myself, so I can learn to fly.

If I had two wishes, and two were all I had,
And they could just be granted, by my Mom and Dad;
I wouldn't ask for money or any store-bought things,

The greatest gifts I'd ask for are simply Roots and Wings.

Contrary to the thoughts presented in this poem, many parents have told me they feel their primary objective as parents is to protect their children. I feel that this type of thinking can actually be harmful to children. I suggest that our job as parents is to prepare our children to be happy, productive adults. Now, I will admit that when your child is born, your primary job is to protect them. But the closer your children get to adulthood, the more you should consider giving them responsibility for their lives and challenging them to find their own solutions to their problems. Whenever my children tell me of a problem they are dealing with, I ask them what they think they ought to do about it. Together we come up with a solution that empowers them to confront the problem and resolve it. I take little responsibility for helping them

72

overcome their problems; consequently, they continually feel challenged to take responsibility for their lives and to increase their sense of control over their destiny. I am consistently impressed with the solutions they create and the courage they have in implementing these solutions.

So how does this relate to leading employees? Raising children is much like leading employees. The first day you hire someone, you are responsible for their success. From that day on I urge you to help them see the power they have within themselves to become more powerful and productive. The challenge is to do it in a way that is not controlling, but provides structure. The key is to tell them what you expect, but let them decide how to get it. Give them ownership. Let them manage their own one hundred square feet. It is also imperative to help them reach beyond the horizons they have set for themselves. I believe that one of a leader's main responsibilities is to see the magnificence in each one of their employees and help them grow into it.

And what does nourishing their actualization have to do with embracing rebellion? If your employees or children are allowed to develop their own dreams, they will tap into what matters most deeply to them. When they do this, they find something inside themselves they are willing to fight for. Remember how hard Mother Teresa fought for her dream? When you nourish the actualization of those around you, you have to be a strong leader; you have to be comfortable with rebellion, because only when people are ready to fight have you tapped into what is most special, insightful, and productive about them. Only then, will they contribute all that they can to their family, their company, and indeed, the world.

Chapter Seven

Establishing Traditions

"A love of tradition has never weakened a nation, indeed it has strengthened nations in their hour of peril."

Winston Churchill

An important part of developing an organization where it is safe to rebel is the establishment of traditions that make people feel they are part of something special. Since Native Americans were masters at developing such traditions, we can look to them for guidance in this area. For example, many Native American tribes had a tradition of doing a dance before they went to a buffalo hunt. What some people may not know is why they did these dances. Joseph Campbell, in his PBS special and DVD, *The Power of Myth* describes how one Native American tribe developed their buffalo hunt tradition. In this particular case, the tradition comes from a mythological story about the relationship between the Indians and the buffalo. I will do my best to recount the story Campbell told in that DVD.

In ancient times the ancestors of this tribe would drive the buffalo off the cliff to provide food and skins for the winter. This one particular year the buffalo would not cooperate and kept turning away from the cliff at the last minute. This was frustrating for the tribe, because they understood that they would have no food if they could not kill some of the buffalo. At this point in the story, one of the young women in the tribe said to the leader of the buffalo, "If your herd will only run off the cliff, I will marry one of you." At that point, the buffalo started coming off the cliff and many were killed upon the rocks below. Unfortunately for the young woman, the leader of the buffalo survived the fall and stood up. He then said, "Okay, young lady, you made a promise, so let's go." The woman was shocked, but felt compelled to honor her promise. Sadly, the young woman went back to the buffalo herd with the understanding that this was where she had to spend the rest of her life.

Her father, the chief, upon hearing what had happened to her, decided to rescue her. He waited until dark and then crept into the herd and whispered into his daughter's ear that he had come to take her back to the tribe. She urged him to leave because she had made a promise and she felt that the buffalo would kill him if they awoke. Sure enough, their conversation awoke the buffalo. The buffalo realized that the chief was trying to take back his daughter, and they became very angry and trampled him to death.

Obviously, the chief's daughter was deeply distraught by this and sat by the remains of her father and wept. The leader of the buffalo, upon seeing this, realized how much the young woman loved her father and asked if there was something they could do to relieve her sorrow. She asked them for a buffalo hide, which they gave her. She laid it over the remains of her father and began to do a dance around it. As she danced, a form of a body began to emerge under the buffalo hide. She looked under the hide and her father was reappearing, but not yet alive. She then danced some more and eventually her father came to life and sat up.

The buffalo were amazed by this and told the young woman she could go back to her tribe with her father under the condition that every time the Indians were going to hunt buffalo, they would perform the dance this young woman had performed for her father. That way the tribe could get the meat they needed for the winter, and the spirits of the deceased buffalo would be allowed to return to their herd where it could be born again, just as her father had been.

This story illustrates the power of tradition in binding a community together. In this case, the tribe was bound together and connected spiritually with the animals they depended upon for their survival every time they did this dance. Through this ritual, they were also able to connect with other members of the tribe and feel they were part of a tradition that had been handed down from past generations. In this ritual they were able to gain a greater sense of their place in the world. In my opinion, finding our place in the world is critical to the process of individualizing ourselves that gives us the strength to rebel, to find our own voice.

This is just one example of the importance of developing traditions in your organization or family. Traditions can give members of your organization or family a sense of connection with one another, can help them appreciate the significance of their work together, and can help them feel they are part of something larger than themselves.

This last point is particularly important in establishing meaning for the individual. The *Dictionary of Team Development Activities* states that most people describe as the highlight of their lives participating on a team that is in pursuit of a goal that is larger than they could have accomplished by themselves. Think about your past. When did you feel most alive? When asked this question, many of us recall stories such as going out in December every year to cut down a Christmas tree with our families, or many other family traditions.

In our family, we have a tradition before we eat dinner together in the evening. Before dinner we all hold hands and give thanks for our day and pray for people we know who are struggling. This prayer is often the springboard for great conversations during dinner. If one of our children prays for a peer at school, we get to hear about what is going on with that classmate during dinner. This often stimulates discussions that go on long after the meal is finished. It helps us develop a sense of community. Interestingly, when I counseled troubled adolescents, I noticed that very few of their families ate dinner together. I believe that this simple tradition can be a great forum for family members to connect with one another.

Traditions can also give us a feeling of stability and safety. In a world that is in fast motion, traditions can give us a sense of stability that we all need for our peace of mind. Religions are probably the best at utilizing the power of traditions. I believe that billions of people attend church partly because of the sense of stability it adds to their lives. It helps them get focused upon what matters in their lives while they connect with those in their spiritual community.

Also, when communication is difficult among members of a family or organization traditions can help us find our place in the organization. I am reminded of a scene in *City Slickers* when Bruno Kirby's character is talking about baseball. He talks about how he and his father had a tradition of always going to baseball games together. When he became a young man and communication with his father became difficult, there was always that tradition to help them feel connected to each other and bridge the gap that naturally occurs when an adolescent is maturing. By taking the time to go to the ballgame with his son, the father of Bruno's character was letting him know that he cared about him, even though talking directly with him was difficult.

Personally, the traditions of one group I was a part of helped me survive one of the most difficult periods of my life. When I was young, I joined the Boy Scouts of America. That organization is steeped in tradition. During this period when I was in scouting, my mother became ill with cancer and eventually died. This whole period was incredibly painful and scary for me. I felt lost a good deal of the time. The traditions of scouting helped me find my place in the world and gave me the stability and sense of community that I needed to survive this period. I can remember how connected I felt to the other members of our troop as we went through the weekly rituals during our meetings. It felt so reassuring at a time when I was so lost that sometimes I did not know how I would get through the day.

Traditions can also help us develop reverence and humility for those who have come before us. They give a sense of where we have come from and an appreciation for our ancestors. For instance, my cousin's family has a Thanksgiving tradition of going out into the woods and building a fire together. This tradition was started decades ago by my uncle. Even though he passed away years ago and all of his children are grown, this tradition continues. It is a way to pay tribute to their father/grandfather and connect with each other.

Another example of the importance of tradition is a holiday that all Americans celebrate. Every Memorial Day our country pays homage to those veterans who have fought and died for our nation. I am always humbled by stories of their courage and appreciative of the sacrifices they have made for their fellow Americans. Whenever I get an opportunity I thank veterans for the sacrifices they have made for our nation. The tradition of Memorial Day gives me a venue to get this in focus. For example, last Memorial Day I drove past a neighbor's yard. In it was sign painted with two words, "Thank you!" On the top of the plywood was an American flag. This simple, but heartfelt expression of thanks to those who have gone before us choked me up. It also made me feel connected to other members of my community.

So how does a company or family start a tradition? The best way is to ask each member of the organization/family what would be meaningful to them. Look around to see what others in similar circumstances are doing. Often traditions start small: a baseball game, building a fire, a get-together at a restaurant. Once your group has an experience that pulls all of you close together, find a way to create a tradition that recreates that closeness on a regular basis. There really is not a wrong way to do this. The whole point is to create an environment where all of you feel connected with each other.

I must add a word of caution. If you are attempting to start a tradition, be sure to keep the focus on building community, not limiting creativity. The danger in starting traditions is that those that may not resonate with them may feel compelled to abide by the tradition even if it feels confining or life-detracting. Leave room for dissenting opinions and have the flexibility to change the tradition based upon the present membership in the group.

You may wonder if there really is a connection between establishing traditions and encouraging people to rebel. To be honest, I don't know if there is. I certainly have never seen any research supporting this notion. But something inside of me tells me that without traditions, we never really develop a sense of community. Without community we never find a place that is safe enough to find out who we really are. As I have said repeatedly in this book, the process of finding our identity necessitates rebellion. Because of their importance in the development of community, I believe traditions have an important place in making your organization a safe place to rebel. I believe this is so because when we know we can come back to a safe place, it's easier to reach out, risk, and explore. It can give one a deep feeling of inner peace to always know we can come home. This inner peace is critical to our ability to rebel and find ourselves.

Chapter Eight

Extending Praise

"People ask you for criticism, but they only want praise."

William Somerset Maugham

So why do employees rebel? Generally, I think it is because they feel unappreciated, undervalued. When I am hired as a consultant, I often interview people in the company to see how they view the problems their organization is having. Almost without exception, I hear stories from employees who say that the only time their boss talks to them is when he/she criticizes them. It all boils down to a feeling on the employees' part that they are laboring so that their boss or the owners can profit -- a situation that would make many of us angry.

Kenneth Kovacks addressed this problem in research he has done over the last fifty years. Once in 1955, and again in 1995, he did surveys in randomly selected companies all over America. He asked managers what they thought motivated their subordinates. They listed the top three motivators in order as follows:

1)   Good wages
2)   Job security
3)   Promotion opportunities

He then asked the subordinates to list their top motivators in order. They were as follows:

1)   Interesting work
2)   Full appreciation for work done
3)   Feeling of being in on things

Interestingly, there are no common items on these lists. Why is it that leaders lose focus on what really matters to employees? What happens to managers after they get promoted? Somehow they seem to forget what motivated them before they assumed their new responsibilities. Often I hear statements similar to these from managers, "These employees cannot be satisfied. I pay them above industry average and they have an unbelievable benefits package, but still they complain. It is impossible to please them!" Sounds kind of like the parent in Chapter One doesn't it? No wonder the employees feel frustrated and misunderstood.

Marcus Buckingham, in his book *First Break all the Rules*, found that the most significant factor determining whether employees are happy in their jobs is their relationship with their supervisor. If you think about it, the way that most of us develop strong relationships with our supervisors is that they show respect for us. They do this by soliciting our opinions, listening to us, and most importantly, by showing appreciation for the contributions we make on the job, that is, praising us. I feel that the power of feeling appreciated cannot be overestimated in making people feel special and helping them maximize their potential.

I can recall one instance when I felt deeply appreciated in my youth and how it has impacted the rest of my life. When I was about twelve years old I took part in a Board of Review to become a First Class Boy Scout. To pass the Board of Review we had to prepare like we were taking a test. We then had an oral exam with several leaders. This process could be pretty intimidating, but I always enjoyed it. I was blessed with good intellect, and I loved performing in front of others (no wonder I'm a consultant!). After I had passed this particular review, one of the members of the board, my Uncle Dick, pulled me aside and told me that he was deeply impressed by my level of mastery of the material I had prepared. He told me that I was unusually gifted and could really make a contribution to the world if I chose to. I remember feeling incredibly valued at that point. I felt like I was walking on air. I can also tell you that his belief in me started a dream in me that today has become my company, Integrated Leadership Systems. There is no telling what any of us can achieve if we feel that our efforts are being noticed by our leaders.

Frederick Herzberg's motivation theory states that factors such as pay, benefits and working conditions are "hygiene" factors in motivation; they are necessary, but not sufficient to motivate. He lists the following as motivating factors: recognition, the work itself, and possibilities for advancement; basically the top of Kovack's employee list. The fact of the matter is few people will work to the best of their ability unless they feel appreciated.

In his book *A Whale of a Tale* Kenneth Blanchard talks about the importance of appreciating employees. He uses the example of killer whales that are trained by Sea World. Anyone who has ever seen these behemoth creatures perform knows it is an amazing sight to behold. How do these trainers, weighing around 200 pounds, motivate these twenty-foot, ten-ton animals? Well, they do not criticize them, ever! They use a technique psychologists call "operant conditioning." That is, any behavior that in any way approximates the behavior the trainer wishes the whale to perform is rewarded with a fish. By doing this, the trainers shape the animal's behavior into the exact behavior they are seeking. As Kenneth Blanchard says, if you really want to motivate your employees, learn to "catch them doing something right; don't criticize them."

Marital research also sheds some light on this situation. In *What Makes Marriages Succeed or Fail,* John Gottman discusses his twenty years of research on what makes the difference between successful and unsuccessful marriages. Can there be a more important team than a marriage? In it, he says that a preponderance of positive experiences is critical to the success of marriage, especially when balanced with a dose of reality. I'm using a little literary license here because I'm assuming that most people would describe feeling appreciated as a positive experience and being criticized as a negative experience. My experience as a marital counselor leads me to believe that feeling unappreciated is a very common problem in most unhappy marriages. At any rate, the key was not whether couples praised or criticized each other; it was the proportion of each that mattered. In the most successful marriages, the proportion of praise to criticism was about four to one. If the percentage of criticism was higher than the percentage of praise, the marriages tended to fail. Interestingly, if the percentage of praise got too high, say ten to one, the marriages also tended to fail, because tough issues were not getting discussed and resolved.

Learning theory also addresses the role of praise in motivation. Over and over, research has proven that rewards make lasting changes to behavior; punishment does not. Rest assured that compliance can be attained with punishment. But you will never develop a spirit of cooperation by using it. You may achieve initial compliance, but your employees will find a way to rebel against you. There are always negative consequences to punishment. Gandhi, having withstood severe punishment from the British government on many occasions said, "They may hit me and break my bones. Then they will have my body, not my obedience."

All of this talk about praise reminds me of an experience I had with my daughter Julie. At the end of January about two years ago, I was coaching my daughter's basketball team. Our record was 0-3 and I was feeling pretty frustrated. Why wouldn't these kids listen? Every time I tried to teach them something new they seemed uninterested. It just didn't seem like they cared about playing hard as a team. I was at a loss as to how to turn the team around.

Then my daughter said to me, "Dad, you are just too intense about this. It's not the Super Bowl, you know." Boy, did I feel like a dummy. After asking my daughter's permission, I asked her teammates if they agreed with her. They did. I asked them what they wanted me to change. They told me I was too critical and I didn't let them play around enough during practice. I was too strict. Interestingly, what I saw as instruction, they saw as criticism. So I made a deal with them. I told them they could do anything they wanted during the first ten minutes of practice as long as they listened to me the last hour and fifty minutes. They cheerfully agreed. After that I stopped criticizing the girls. Instead, if I saw someone doing something wrong, I looked for someone who was doing it right and stopped practice and made a big deal showing everyone how wonderfully this person was performing her duties. Meanwhile, everyone else got the lesson I was trying to teach and no one's feelings were hurt. So did this help our results? I'll say. We won our next game 23-6. In fact, we won all of our games leading up to the championship of the league, where we barely lost to a team that had beaten us by twenty points earlier in the season. Many parents commented to me after our games that they were impressed with how well our girls were playing as a team. Amazing, the wisdom of children. It also points out how blind we can be to the effects of our behavior upon others and the need to seek feedback.

Throughout this chapter, I have talked about the value of praise in motivating employees. I believe it is even more critical when raising children. You may anger an adult by criticizing, but you can do irreparable damage to a child by doing so. I believe that our main job as parents is to give our children self-esteem. Developmental research at The Ohio State University would support this notion. This research indicates that as long as children grow up with a good self-image, parents can make a whole host of other mistakes and the kids still become well-adapted adults.

Also, in his book *Mastery,* George Leonard talks about research Tom Peters, author of *In Search of Excellence*, did with the most successful businessmen. Tom Peters described an "eerily similar set of circumstances" in the homes of the children who grow up to become high-level leaders. He says the parents of these children "praised them to the point of embarrassment." This may seem like overdoing it, but I believe that each child is sacred. If we, as parents, can help them to understand this, I believe they will become happy and successful.

In a recent speech, Denis Waitley, author of *The Psychology of Winning*, told how he suggests helping children understand how special they are. Allow me to paraphrase. "When your children get in bed at night, and all of the distractions are out of the way, get them in a straightjacket with the sheets and covers of their bed and look into their eyes and gently say, 'Hey, I've been watching you, and I think you are just about the most amazing person I have ever met. I just want you to know how proud I am to be your parent. I love you so much.'" What child would not feel special upon hearing this every night? No doubt, praise is critical in making people feel special and helping them find their voice.

Similar to my point in the last chapter regarding traditions, praising our employees or children makes them feel special. It helps them develop the inner strength to really value their own opinions. Once individuals know that they have something important to contribute, they will fight to make that contribution, even if they have to rebel.

Chapter Nine

Leading Women

"Well behaved women rarely make history."

Laurel Thatcher Ulrich

Two years ago I took a three hundred and sixty degree leadership assessment profile. The results showed that when I become insecure, I behave in an arrogant fashion. I really did not like hearing this about myself, so as usual I took the results to my family to ask if this was true. When I asked my fifteen year-old daughter, Molly, she began to cry. "What is going on?" I asked. "I am so happy to hear you say that," she replied. "All of my life I have assumed you are right about everything. When you have behaved arrogantly, I have always felt that my feelings didn't matter. It made me feel small and weak. You seemed so sure of yourself that I assumed I didn't know what I was talking about. What a relief to hear that this is your problem. It gives me a surge of self-worth!"
Wow. I have always been a proponent of seeking honest feedback, but I did not expect to hear that from my daughter. Little did I know how my insecurity was harming her. Boy, did I feel stupid!
Evidently, Molly's feelings of inadequacy are not unusual for teenage girls. Mary Pipher, Ph.D., in her groundbreaking book, *Reviving Ophelia* talks about how many teenage girls are lost in this same fog, unable to determine who they are surrounded by a world that constantly tells them to

behave in ways counter to what would be healthy for them. I think that most men have no idea of the pressure women are under. I'm not sure that I do either, but I am trying. Everywhere in the media women are portrayed as sexual objects. In school, there are constant messages to young women that they will succeed based upon the relationships they develop, not upon their accomplishments. Many young women report feeling that they have a choice between becoming professionally successful or getting married. They report that they receive constant feedback that assertive behavior and independence, the very traits young men are encouraged to develop, are not feminine and should not be pursued. Many young women become overwhelmed by this situation. Many never resolve it. In fact, I recently spoke with a female colleague who said that practically every woman she has coached in leadership positions is plagued by self-doubt, and those are the successful women.

Many men reading this chapter may wonder why I am focusing upon the adolescent lives of women. "Aren't they grown up now? Haven't they gotten over all of this?" Research would suggest that many of them have not. Actually, none of us ever does completely. While it's not your job as a manager to see that they move through this stage of development, it will benefit both of you if you are able to support the women who work for you as they face these challenges. The research I referred to above, which was also mentioned earlier in this book, suggests that up to eighty percent of us never fully leave this adolescent stage of development.

The stage of adolescence I am referring to is called the dependent stage by Robert Kegan, a noted Harvard University psychologist and the author of *The Evolving Self: Problem and Process in Human Development*. This stage is accompanied by the belief that "I only matter if others think I matter, and belonging to a group is more important than being myself." I feel it is the job of leaders to assist all of their employees through this dependent stage to the next stage, independence. However, a "one-size-fits-all" mentality does not work here. What works for men generally will not work for women. In my opinion, learning this fact is a big part of becoming an effective leader of women. If you really want women to tell you what they think, to encourage their rebellion, you have to learn to lead them in a way that encourages their independence.

I turn again to the research of Eric Erikson. As I mentioned earlier, Dr. Erikson listed eight stages that human beings progress through on their road to adulthood. In each stage a conflict must be resolved for the individual to proceed to the next stage. In stage five, "Identity versus Role Confusion," the individual feels intense pressure to belong to a group. This stage typically happens during adolescence. To add confusion, at this same time they are expected to start establishing their own identities. Also, they are for the first time dealing with sexual hormones, which can be overwhelming. This is the age where individuals first realize there are just so many partners and jobs to go around, and they must successfully compete for them. All of this can be extremely difficult for them to process. In fact, my sixteen-year-old daughter often tells me that she wonders if she will ever be able to find a job when she gets out of college, even though she has an "A" average at one of the best private schools in Ohio.

In general, I feel that many men do not understand what motivates women. Because of this, I believe there is a huge opportunity for male managers to improve their organizations by learning to lead women more effectively. Allow me to give an example of a man, Anson Dorrance, who appears to understand the difference between motivating men and women. He is the men's and women's soccer coach at the University of North Carolina. His women's teams have won eighteen national championships. He feels that male players are more motivated by being challenged to excel. Women, on the other hand, are motivated by the feeling of belonging to a group of women they are proud to associate with.

For example, when Coach Dorrance would see lackluster play on the men's team, he would come into the locker room at half-time and yell at the players. He said every player would think to himself, "Yeah, you bunch of slackers, get on the ball! If you don't start playing harder, we're going to lose this game. I'm going to go out in the second half and show the rest of the team and the coach how it is done."

Early on in his career, he used the same strategy with the women, with poor results. When he challenged the women, they would think to themselves, "I've let my teammates and the coach down. I'm not a very good player. I'm not sure I belong here." The women would become discouraged. Same behavior on the coach's part; different reaction from the players.

Coach Dorrance subsequently learned how to motivate women. Now when the team plays poorly, he goes into the locker room and asks them how they feel they played in the first half. They usually make an accurate assessment of the situation. Then he asks them what they feel they should do to improve their performance in the second half. They work as a team to come up with a solution. They feel like they belong and they feel they own the results; consequently, they generally play better in the second half. Women don't respond to challenges like men do. They like to be shown the problem and decide for themselves how to deal with it, especially when they can do so with other members of a group.

Coach Dorrance gave another example. When he first started coaching the women he would have them jog on the track together to warm up for practice. After about ten years, he eliminated this ritual because he felt like it wasted time. The women players became upset with him. They brooded and played poorly in games and seemed unmotivated in practice.

When he asked them what the problem was, they told him they needed the warm-up as a way to connect with each other, a way to switch from a classroom mentality to a soccer practice mentality. At that point he let them do the warm-up runs again. High levels of performance followed. The take-home lesson is that women want time to connect with each other, to form a sense of community, if they are to perform at high levels. I also feel this community feeling gives women the confidence to fight for what they believe in, that is, rebel.

Men may be reading this and thinking, "There's not that much difference between us, maybe women just haven't learned how to toughen up." That is the precise attitude that frustrates women. When I was working toward my Ph.D. in psychology, I took a class in multicultural psychology. In it our instructor, Fred Leong, said that it was impossible for those responsible for creating the norms in a culture to understand how it feels to be a minority in that culture. This goes for ethnic minorities and women in the workplace. He said it was like the dominant culture is a light bulb. Only those who must operate within the light cast by the bulb can understand its effect upon them. The light bulb itself, in this case men, cannot understand what it is like to work in an environment created by them. Therefore, the only way to really motivate women is to ask them what matters to them and try to adjust our behavior accordingly.

Obviously, we live in a male-dominated work culture. Women have been a significant part of this culture for only a few decades, and they hold relatively few positions of power. When I coach women leaders, they regularly complain about the pressure they feel in the workplace to become something they are not in order to satisfy their boss. For a long time men have tried to force their motivational paradigm upon women in the workplace. Maybe it is time for men to start listening. In the end, I believe we will all benefit. In fact, when one looks at the violence that is rampant all over the world, I think that more than ever this planet needs to hear the voice of women, the voice of kindness, compromise, and understanding.

Women, in general, are socialized not to speak up. They are valued for the problems they solve, not the ones they create. Sometimes creating problems is precisely what your family or organization needs. As noted at the beginning of this chapter, Laurel Thatcher Ulrich once said, "Well behaved women rarely make history." That sounds to me like an invitation to rebel. I think it is the responsibility of the person leading women to create a safe place for them to not be "well behaved," but to rebel.

Chapter Ten

Leading Men

*"A young man is so strong, so mad, so certain, and so lost.
He has everything and he is able to use nothing."*

Thomas Wolfe, *Of Time and the River*

Some men reading the last chapter may feel like, "It's too bad women aren't more like me, direct, confident, and independent. They would be a lot easier to manage." Well, perceptions like those are probably just as inaccurate as the perception that women can be motivated the same way that men can. Henry David Thoreau once said that "the mass of men lead lives of quiet desperation." I think he was right. It is estimated that up to nine million Americans are alcoholics, and two–thirds of them are men. According to The American Association of Suicidology, suicide is the eighth leading cause of death in the United States, about thirty thousand per year. Of those, eighty percent are men. Most of them die having left no warning. How alone they must have felt!

Often, when I worked with male clients as a psychologist, I had a very difficult time getting them to express their negative emotions, except anger. Searching for reasons for this, I would hear stories about fathers who had decades before told their sons to stop acting like girls whenever they expressed sadness or empathy for others. The message became clear to these young men: "If I allow myself to feel these feelings, I risk losing my father's approval." The saddest thing is that this message gets so deep into the psyches of these young men that they are unaware it is there, even decades later. The results can be devastating. When I would see these same men in couples counseling their wives would constantly complain about how emotionally distant their husbands were. The husband would ask for an example and she would say that he would never admit to being afraid, for instance. His reply was often something like, "At my age, I don't feel fear any more." Usually, it took a lot of work with male clients for them to understand that fear was as natural as any other emotion. Once these men became comfortable expressing all of their emotions, including fear, they were able to improve their relationships with their wives.

Why do so many men numb their feelings, and how does this impact their lives and our approach to leading them? Why do they learn to bury their feelings and isolate themselves from those around them? Besides my own life experience and my exposure to hundreds of male clients in my psychology practice, most of the information I will cite in this chapter is from a wonderful book on this subject, entitled *Raising Cain, Protecting the Emotional Life of Boys* by Daniel Kindlon and Michael Thompson. In it the authors state, "We believe that boys, beginning at a young age, are systematically steered away from their emotional lives toward silence, solitude, and distrust."

This was absolutely the case in my own upbringing. From a young age I was encouraged to stifle my feelings and "act like a man." I can recall one instance when my brother was crying and my father mocked him for about thirty minutes as he cried. It left a deep impression upon me. I decided I would never risk such humiliation from my father. I learned not to cry. In fact I can remember one ten-year stretch when I did not cry. Believe it or not, now I cry several times per week. It is so cleansing. But at age fourteen, when my mother died, I was unable to process many of my feelings because they made me feel weak. We, as a society, have held up men like John Wayne as role models – strong, independent, apparently never experiencing doubt. Unfortunately, I bought into this thinking. Only later in life did I find out that John Wayne was a poor husband and father, and he struggled with alcohol dependence; not much of a role model. Regardless, the damage had been done. As I began to struggle with the challenges of my developing manhood, I became increasingly overwhelmed with feelings I did not know how to process. Unfortunately, my response to feeling overwhelmed was to expend increasing amounts of energy trying to convince others that I had no problems. Eventually there was little emotional energy left to deal with my problems. Also, unbeknownst to me, by acting like everything was fine, I was cutting myself off from the very people who could have helped me.

If you do nothing else for your sons or men who work for you, I urge you to help them understand that processing all of their emotions, positive and negative, is necessary for their happiness and fulfillment. Kindlon and Thompson state that the bulk of their work in aiding dysfunctional young men is to "help them understand their emotional life and develop an emotional vocabulary." In too many men, the only negative emotion that can be expressed is anger. Any expression of vulnerability is discouraged for men as they grow older. How is a person supposed to learn to rebel in an effective way if they are not allowed to tap into their feelings, to get in touch with the things in their environment that make them feel frustrated, devalued, or powerless? Yes, understanding our emotions as men is critical to finding our voice and learning to fight for what we believe in. Good leadership can help us do this.

What is interesting about this problem is that many men feel that it is weak to express fear. In fact, many men have a bumper sticker on their vehicles that says "No Fear." I think a much more functional statement is "Know Fear." I'm scared about something every day. For instance last spring my doctor indicated to me that my blood work suggested that I might have cancer. I spent a month wondering about this before I was given a clean bill of health. As my father's health continues to decline, I feel sad and afraid to say goodbye to him for the last time. Every time my daughter takes the car and arrives home late, I experience a little fear. I have learned that fear is a natural emotion. It occurs whenever we, or someone we love, is threatened. It is necessary for our survival. Many men feel that people who are courageous are never afraid. I think the opposite is true. In the words of Dan Millman, "Courage is not the absence of fear, but the conquering of it." But you have to be willing to admit that you are afraid before you can be courageous.

So what is a leader of men supposed to do? How do you help them through this? And, how do you parent a young man? In my opinion, the answer is the same, you help them wrestle with and learn to understand their emotions. According to Kindlon and Thompson, "Boys need an emotional vocabulary that expands their ability to express themselves in ways other than anger or aggression." In fact, when researchers compare men and women on their emotional awareness, men almost invariably finish second. I don't think that outcome is necessary. If we as parents/leaders can allow the men under our supervision the freedom to explore and process their emotions, they can be just as emotionally functional as women. I also think this emotional intelligence that they gain will pay huge dividends to their families and organizations as they learn to harness what they are passionate about and face their fears.

You may be thinking, well, "Perhaps boys just don't have as much emotion as girls do." Actually, the opposite appears to be true. In an intriguing study by Richard Fabes and Nancy Eisenburg, researchers played a tape of a baby crying to young boys and girls and monitored their physiological reactions. The results showed that the boys were more upset by the crying than the girls. It is also interesting to note that while the girls appeared to deal with their discomfort, the boys did everything in their power to avoid dealing with the distressing sounds. In the words of Kindlon and Thompson, "boys who have trouble managing their own emotions may routinely tune out the cues of other people's upset."

Michael Riera in the book, *The Roller Coaster Years,* cites research by Michael Guirian who states, "The female brain processes more emotive stimulants, through more senses, and more completely than does the male. It also verbalizes emotive information quickly. Boys can sometimes take hours to process emotively (and manage the same information as girls). This lesser emotive ability makes males more emotionally fragile than we tend to think." Riera goes on to state that since girls tend to be more emotive than boys, not only do they get to process the emotions, but because boys don't look as emotionally vulnerable, we are more likely to miss or overlook a boy in emotional distress. So, as boys grow older and this tendency is reinforced by social norming, some men can become emotional time bombs with a great deal of unprocessed emotions. This is compounded because no one knows they are in pain. They are on an emotional island, and asking for help is just too vulnerable to consider.

One of the reasons that men have difficulty expressing their emotions is that their parents more harshly discipline them. According to Kindlon and Thompson, corporal punishment was still used in eighty-five percent of homes as recently as 1985. This behavior is most often targeted at boys. A recent study found that boys were fifty percent more likely to be physically abused than girls, and fathers were much more likely to hit a teenage son than a teenage daughter. While fathers may think this toughens up their sons, the actual effect is more likely to be shame, self-hatred, and anger. Also, with no way to express these feelings, these wounded young men often grow up to be angry, depressed adults.

I believe that another responsibility for leaders of men is to be a model of emotional attachment. This especially applies to male leaders. Few people will follow if you do not model the behavior you are seeking. Once again, if you are not sure of your level of emotionally intelligence, I suggest you consider reading *Emotional Intelligence* and *Primal Leadership* by Daniel Goleman. These books will give you some excellent ideas about what emotional intelligence is and how to develop it. When you talk to your male subordinates or children, don't be afraid to express your feelings with them. Show empathy for their feelings. Herb Albert once said, "One of the keys to dealing with artists is to be sensitive to their feelings and their needs, to give them their day in court so they can air their grievances or their brilliant ideas." I believe the same could be said about leading men. Help your male employees understand that it is not a weakness, but a strength to need others' help sometimes. No one is an island. Teams work best when members understand that they need each other to accomplish the team's goals. Let them know it's okay not to have the answers. And don't criticize them for making mistakes; rather, help them learn from them.

It may seem to some people that by encouraging men to understand their emotions, I am developing a recipe for men who cannot face their own problems. Far from it; I am suggesting just the opposite. As you help your male employees understand their emotions they will learn to overcome the ones that are holding them back as they learn to harness the passion they need to become great contributors on your team. I am asking you to give your male employees the power to feel and constructively express all of their emotions. This process is necessary for them to understand what they deeply care about. It is also a vital piece of their learning to understand any emotions, like fear, that may be blocking their actualization.

Once they deeply understand and can harness their emotions, watch out. There will be no stopping them.

Once again, be forewarned that the process men go through in giving themselves permission to feel all of their emotions is a bumpy one. Letting out long-repressed emotions is not an exact science. It can get messy. It can take the form of rebellion. But if you, as a leader, are comfortable embracing this rebellion, the payoff to you and those men who report to you will be significant.

Final Thoughts

"We must not cease from exploration. And the end of all our exploring will be to arrive where we began and to know the place for the first time."

T.S. Elliot

Throughout this book, I have suggested that embracing rebellion can be a difficult choice to make, but I believe the results will be well worth your effort. When you really get down to it, every time we refuse to embrace the rebellion around us, it is because of our own insecurity. I also believe that our main journey on this Earth is to become the person the Creator intended us to be and then to give that person fully to those around us. I believe that embracing rebellion is a key part of completing that mission.

I hope you have benefited from reading this book. I hope that it assisted you in your journey toward better leadership. If you are interested in finding more resources to continue your development, or that of your team consider contacting me at:

Integrated leadership Systems, LLC
3805 N. High St., Suite 310
Columbus, OH 43214
614-784-8530
www.integratedleader.com

About the author

Steve Anderson earned his undergraduate degree from The Ohio State University in Agricultural Business in 1980. He subsequently worked in several positions in the agriculture and retail industries. He achieved his Masters in Business Administration from Capital University in Columbus, Ohio in 1995. He attained his Ph.D. in Counseling Psychology from The Ohio State University in 1999. He is a licensed Psychologist. Since graduating, he has developed his consulting business, Integrated Leadership Systems, LLC. His focus in this business is to help organizations achieve their maximum potential by helping their members become more authentic leaders. He lives with his family in Columbus, Ohio.